True Tales of Heroes & Heroines

Valerie Marsh

Illustrated by Patrick K. Luzadder

Alleyside
Press®

Fort Atkinson, Wisconsin

This book is about people who started out as ordinary individuals but had an extraordinary desire to help others. Each of us is just one person, but one person can truly make a difference.

To the hero or heroine in each of us: Go out and make a difference of one!

Published by Alleyside Press,
an imprint of Highsmith Press LLC
Highsmith Press
W5527 Highway 106
P.O. Box 800
Fort Atkinson, Wisconsin 53538-0800
1-800-558-2110

© Valerie Marsh, 1999
Cover design: Frank Neu

The paper used in this publication meets the minimum requirements of American National Standard for Information Science — Permanence of Paper for Printed Library Material. ANSI/NISO Z39.48-1992.

Library of Congress Cataloging-in-Publication Data
Marsh, Valerie.
    True tales of heroes & heroines / Valerie Marsh ; illustrated by
Patrick K. Luzadder.
      p. cm.
    Includes bibliographical references.
    ISBN 0-917846-93-1 (pbk. : alk. paper)
    1. Biography--Study and teaching. 2. United States--Biography-
-Study and teaching. 3. Storytelling--United States.   I. Luzadder,
Patrick K.   II. Title.   III. Title: True tales of heroes and heroines.
CT85.M37 1999
920.02--dc21
                                    98-48774
                                     CIP

Contents

Introduction 5

Stories

✂ Alexander Graham Bell 8

✂ Nellie Bly 12

✎ Louis Braille 17

🖼 Andrew Carnegie 21

🖼 Roberto Clemente 25

✂ Walt Disney 29

✎ Terry Fox 33

🏠 Florence Kelley 37

✋ Juliette Low 41

✂ Maria Montessori 45

✋ Mother Teresa 49

✋ John Muir 53

🏠 Louis Pasteur 57

🖼 Princess Diana 61

🖼 Christopher Reeve 65

✂ Eleanor Roosevelt 68

🏠 Albert Schweitzer 73

✂ Sequoyah 77

✎ Harriet Tubman 81

✂ Raoul Wallenberg 85

Story Method Directions 90

Story Method Icons

Paper-Cutting   Mystery-Fold   Sign Language   Storyknifing   Story Puzzles

*"I am only one; but still I am one. I cannot do everything,
but still I can do something.
I will not refuse to do the something I can do."*
Helen Keller

*"I don't know what your destiny will be, but one thing I know:
the only ones among you who will be really happy are those who
have sought and found how to serve."*
Albert Schweitzer

*"Once or twice in a lifetime, someone special comes along who
touches our hearts, deepens our faith in humanity and
changes forever the way we look at the world.
Someone who exhibits courage, selflessness and tenacity—someone who
fights for a dream and works to make it come true.
They speak to us of goodness and possibilities, of defiance
in the face of an enemy, of human decency
and most of all generosity."*
Excerpt from Terry Fox Foundation brochure

"The happiest people are those who do the most for others."
Booker T. Washington

"Only a life lived for others is the life worthwhile."
Albert Einstein

"A man's true wealth is the good he does in the world."
Mohammed

"Jesus said love one another. He didn't say love the whole world."
Mother Teresa

Introduction

Children need heroes! Adults need heroes! They give us inspiration and guidance in an ever-changing world. How much richer we are, all because of our heroes and heroines.

A heroine might be a person who risks her life to save someone in danger. A hero can be someone who overcomes great physical or personal odds in order to accomplish his dream. Or a hero can be a person who becomes a celebrity because he possesses a single, great, and often unusual skill. Finally, a hero can be someone who does something that no one else has ever done before, such as climb the highest mountain.

Then there are heroes whose greatness develops over a lifetime. Their heroism is demonstrated in their courage, commitment, and high ideals. These people each have a *particular,* often impossible, goal, requiring years of tireless dedication and hard work. Sometimes their efforts are recognized and sometimes they are not. However pleasant, recognition and reward are not their goals. They experience life fully and they make mistakes, just like everyone else.

The heroes in this book include people involved in science, the arts, medicine, business, education, government, religion, public and private life. Each has given something remarkable to society. Each had the ability to see or do things in a new way. With their commitment, determination, and actions, these individuals showed what can be accomplished with extraordinary personal sacrifice against daunting odds. They showed that tremendous change can occur when one person has a vision and the courage to follow it.

The world is changing at an ever increasing rate and today, more than ever, young people need to find role models in the people who have gone before them. Learning about heroes helps young people in many ways:

- Real heroes can fire up a listener's imagination. We can often relate to some of the challenges that a hero has faced.

- A role model with high standards can encourage children, and adults, to reach for greater heights.

- Heroes can help build character and show us how one should live one's life.

- Knowledge of heroes helps develop citizenship skills.

- Using their knowledge of real-life heroes, young people can more intelligently explore the choices that

have been given to them and make wise decisions for themselves.

Therefore, it is important for us as educators, storytellers, and parents to recognize that we are in the unique position of becoming a hero to a child, even though we might not even know that a child views us as his hero.

Hopefully, this awareness brings out the best in us and inspires us. But some days it takes courage just to go about our daily routine at home and at work! We deal the best we can with the expected and unexpected challenges that come our way and that is heroic enough!

That we find ourselves challenged and inspired by stories of heroes proves that there is a hero in every one of us. We do have the power to change things, and we can always strive to use our unique talents to help create a better world for ourselves and for others.

As you read these stories about special individuals, hopefully you and your listeners will see something of yourself in each of them.

Storytelling Methods

In this book, you will find a variety of storytelling methods. Using these methods makes your stories more interesting for your listeners.

Paper-cutting stories involve telling a story while cutting a piece of folded paper. At the end of the story, unfold the paper to reveal your surprise object.

Mystery-fold stories involve drawing a picture and then folding the paper together at the end of your story to create a surprise picture.

Sign language stories are told with key words in sign language so that listeners can join in the telling with you.

Story puzzles are tangram puzzle pieces that are used to make simple shapes to enhance the story.

Storyknifing is a simple drawing method used to pique the listener's interest.

Each of these storytelling methods interprets an individual story in an interesting, and often dramatic way. Directions, patterns and other helpful information on each is located in the Story Method Directions at the back of the book (p. 90). You can choose your favorite storytelling method and then tell those stories with that method. Or you can choose a favorite hero or heroine and tell that story.

Activities to Use with the Stories

There are suggested activities and discussion questions with each story in this book. The following are some additional suggestions for enriching story sessions:

1. Give children an opportunity to tell the stories! Divide the responsibility for reading each story among the children, while you do the paper-cutting, sign language, or other special storytelling techniques.

2. Discuss how the challenges that the hero or heroine overcame were unique to the time in history when the person lived. Children need to learn about a wide variety of interesting people from all walks of life. This expands their knowledge base of the time period when the person lived, and the particular challenges of those times. For example, Harriet Tubman was faced with the problem of slavery. Louis Braille was faced with the public's general apathy toward people with disabilities.

3. Discuss how a particular hero could use today's technology to further her cause. For example, Florence Kelly might have appeared on a television news show to discuss her cause. Maria Montessori might have kept her teaching colleagues updated with e-mail. Nellie Bly could have faxed her newspaper articles to her publisher as she travelled around the world.

4. List ten advancements that society has made since a particular hero was alive. These could be in the areas of science, medicine, transportation, communication, etc. Next to each improvement, discuss or write down how this particular improvement would have affected the hero's life.

5. Have children make a "Bio Bag" by decorating a paper bag with facts about the famous person. Include date of birth, place of birth, family members, a picture of the heroine, a picture of their home or place of work and two interesting facts about them. Then put several objects in the bag that represent the hero.

Children could present their "Bio Bag" project to other listeners. First, they could explain the outside of the bag. Then they could pull one object out of their bag and tell why the object represents the hero. For example, put a book in a bag to represent Andrew Carnegie. Use a crown or a piece of fancy costume jewelry to represent Princess Diana. For Alexander Graham Bell, use a very small battery to represent part of a hearing aid.

6. Dress up in a costume representative of the hero. Choose a hero who is easy to do! Explain your costume and props to your listeners. Then tell the story.

7. Hold a weekly "Guess Who? Contest." Read a clue about the heroine each morning. Encourage the students to write down their guesses and put them in the "Heroes Box."

At the end of the week, read all of the clues again and then announce the winner. This could be the first person who guessed correctly. If you have more than one correct guess, announce all the winners. Or you could draw one name from all the correct guesses. Ask the winner(s) to tell who the hero was and perhaps give other information about this hero. Award a small prize to the winner. For fun, you can include famous people, but also consider local celebrities or people in your school!

9. Cut out paper bricks or use real blocks with paper taped over them to build a "Tower of Facts." After telling the story about the hero, discuss and write one important fact about them on each brick. Stack them in a tower or build a house with them on a bulletin board.

For an extra challenge, after you have studied and made bricks for two or three heroes, mix up or pin the bricks on the bulletin board in random order and see if the students can sort them correctly.

10. Do a bulletin board of "Who, What, Where, When and Why" with your heroes. Add one fact a day, and finally add the name and picture of your heroine. Did they guess it before you put the picture up?

Using the Story Body to Develop Story Ideas

Divide the class into groups of six and let each group choose a hero or heroine to study. After briefly discussing the elements of a story, give each child an enlarged photocopy of one of the pieces of the body that appears on page 7. Children may work together or individually to find the answers to the questions.

Then they cut the pieces out and glue their hero together on a large piece of paper. Using the information on the body, they may give an oral report on their heroine. Bodies may also be used as a rough draft for a final written report.

Story Body

CHARACTER

1. What strengths does the hero have?

_____

_____

2. How does the hero feel about the problem? _____

_____

_____

PROBLEM

What is the problem? (A situation that the hero tries to improve for other people.)

1. _____

_____

_____

2. _____

_____

_____

METHOD

1. How does the hero solve or try to solve the problem? What are the hero's actions or decisions that help solve the problem?

SOLUTION

1. What is the ideal solution?

2. What does the hero want to have happen?

TIME

1. When does the hero live?

2. What was the world like?

SETTING

1. Where does the hero live?

2. Where does he travel in an attempt to solve his problem?

Alexander Graham Bell

Telephones are a very important part of our everyday lives. We use them to call our friends and family, and to get help in an emergency. We often take them for granted, and most homes have more than one telephone. You can find telephones almost everywhere, from airplanes to shopping centers. **(Fold at Fold Line.)**

Think for a minute about how many telephones you have in your house. Perhaps you even have a cellular phone. Today, millions of people make millions of telephone calls to millions of other people all over the world. **(Cut from 1 to 2. Unfold circle as world.)**

I bet you don't remember the very first words that you spoke on the telephone. When you were very small, maybe about three years old, your mother probably let you speak on the telephone to your grandparents or some other relative. It was probably very exciting for you because, like all little children, you were fascinated by the telephone. Today, you probably don't get too excited about using it.

Do you know what the very first words spoken over the first telephone were? Do you know who spoke them?

In Boston, Alexander Graham Bell invented the telephone after years of work.

He had studied human speech and hearing since he was a small boy. He used his knowledge of the human ear and voice box to invent the telephone. In 1876, he used his invention for the very first time to call his assistant. He said, "Watson, come here. I want to see you."

You would think that Mr. Bell would have planned something more exciting to say for the very first telephone conversation. But this we will never know. What we do know, is that Mr. Bell had just spilled battery acid and it was burning a hole through his pants to his leg. He needed Mr. Watson's help in cleaning up the mess quickly.

Alexander Graham Bell used the money that he made from inventing the telephone to help many deaf children. Mr. Bell was an inventor by night and a teacher of deaf children by day. He taught them how to speak, how to use sign language and how to read lips. It bothered him that deaf people, especially children, were so isolated from the rest of the world. **(Cut from 3 to 4.)**

Deafness was a very important part of Mr. Bell's life. His mother was deaf and so was his wife, Mabel. Both his father and his grandfather were teachers of the deaf.

Bell began teaching at age sixteen while he was still living in England. He continued to teach after he moved to America. His most well-known student was Helen Keller. As her teacher, he helped her so much that she dedicated her autobiography to him. Even after Alexander Graham Bell became famous, he continued to work with the deaf, establishing schools for deaf children and setting up institutions for teachers of deaf children.

One school that he opened in Washington, D.C., had a classroom of six deaf children and a classroom of kindergarten children. The children played and ate together. Bell believed that deaf children would learn many things better and faster if they associated with hearing children. Today, many children who are deaf are in regular school classrooms. Mr. Bell was right, some children do learn better this way.

Bell also invented an instrument that could measure how well people could hear, called an audiometer. With an audiometer, minor hearing losses could be detected and children with hearing problems could be helped sooner. You may have taken this test in school.

Mr. Bell had many interests in addition to sound. He also designed the tetrahedron, a pyramid-like shape made up of smaller triangles. It is so strong that tetrahedral designs are used by engineers today to design bridges, sport stadiums and other large open structures. They are called space frames. First, Mr. Bell used his tetrahedral shape to build very large, yet lightweight kites. Then he applied his knowledge to improving the design of airplanes.

After that, he designed hydrofoils—or boats that skim across the surface of the water on a cushion of air.

He established an association called the Alexander Graham Bell Association for the Deaf. This association provides information, counseling and scholarships.

Although he helped many deaf people, Bell wished that he could have done even more.

While people associate Bell with the telephone, he was very proud of his other accomplishments. He said, "Recognition of my work for and interest in the education of the deaf has always been more pleasing to me than recognition of my work with the telephone."

When he died in 1922, ten million telephones were in use, and many of Bell's other inventions were making lives easier and safer. To honor him, all telephone service was stopped for one full minute across the country during Alexander Graham Bell's funeral. **(Cut from 5 to 6. Unfold "1" to represent one minute.)**

Thomas Edison praised his friend and said that he "brought the human family in closer touch."

On Bell's gravestone are the words, "Citizen of the United States and Teacher of the Deaf." This is how he wanted to be remembered. **(Cut from 7 to 8.)**

Today Alexander Graham Bell's own words help us remember him. He said, "An inventor is a man who looks around the world and is not content with things as they are. He wants to improve whatever he sees; he wants to benefit the world."

Alexander Graham Bell was one man who set out to help the world in the best way that he knew how. He made a difference of one. **(Unfold paper to reveal an early Bell desk telephone.)**

- -

Activities & Discussion Questions

1. Alexander Graham Bell changed the world with his inventions. Can you name other inventors and something that they invented?

2. If you could invent anything in the world that would help make life easier for someone, what would you invent?

3. Your home is filled with inventions to make work and play faster, easier and more fun. What is your favorite invention in the kitchen? What is your favorite invention in your living room?

4. Many people who are deaf or who have poor hearing wear hearing aids. Can you think of any library or Internet resources where you can find out how many persons wear hearing aids?

Super Search Question

1. When Alexander Graham Bell invented the telephone, what was the population of the U.S. according to the most recent census? *(Answer: He invented the telephone in 1876; and the census is done every ten years, so the most recent was in 1870. The U.S. population was 39.8 million in 1870.)* What is the population of the U.S. today according to the Census Bureau? *(Answer: For most current estimate check the population clock at www.census.gov/)*

To learn more about Alexander Graham Bell

Websites

► Alexander Graham Bell's Kids Page
http://www.e-znet.com/kids/AlexBellLinks.html

This website provides many links to learning activities on the telephone, biographies on Alexander Graham Bell, and histories of the telephone. From Pasadena Online

► Alexander Graham Bell Institute
http://bell.uccb.ns.ca/
Historical information on the Bell family and the telephone, including many photographs and a children's activities page. From University College of Cape Breton.

► Alexander Graham Bell National Historical Site
http://fortress.uccb.ns.ca/parks/agb_e.html
Provides access to information about the museum established to honor Bell and his work. From the Louisbourg Institute.

Books

Lewis, Cynthia Copeland. *Hello, Alexander Graham Bell Speaking.* Dillon Press, 1991.

MacLeod, Elizabeth. *Alexander Graham Bell: An Inventive Life.* Kids Can Press, 1999. Creative, curious and compassionate, Bell was a remarkable man with an amazing lifetime career. This book chronicles his life, from his childhood in Edinburgh, Scotland, to his work with the hearing-impaired in Boston, up until his death in Nova Scotia in 1922. Full-color photos.

Mathews, Tim. *Always Inventing.* National Geographic, 1999. Period photographs as well as pages from Bell's original notebooks help paint a vivid portrait of the man who—from his first invention at age 11 (a tool to clean husks from wheat kernels) to his patent on hydrofoil improvements 64 years later—was always inventing.

Pasachoff, Naomi. *Alexander Graham Bell: Making Connections.* Oxford Press, 1998. Written for teens. Several sections clearly explain the principles of acoustics, electromagnetism, and the workings of the telephone.

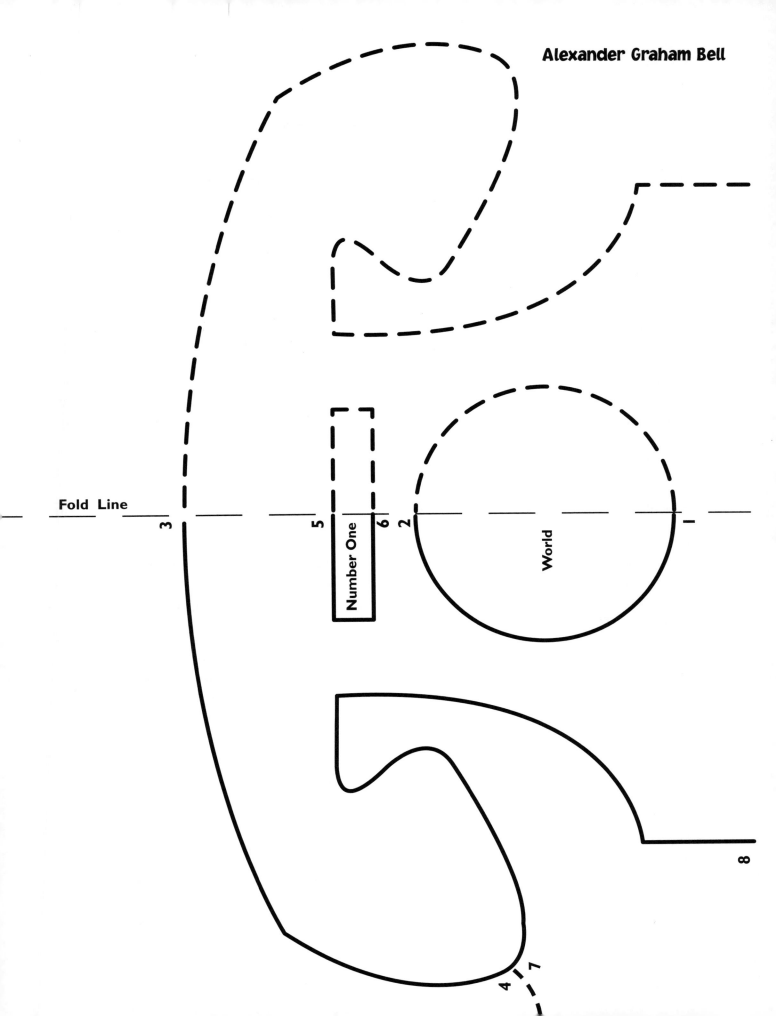

Alexander Graham Bell

Fold Line

3

5

6

2

Number One

World

1

8

4

7

NELLIE BLY

Have you ever wished that your mom or dad had given you a different name? If you could pick any name in the world, what name would you pick?

Back in 1885, there was a girl who changed her name from Elizabeth Cochrane to Nellie Bly. Elizabeth chose the name Nellie Bly because Nellie was a girl in a popular song written by Stephen Foster.

But the main reason she changed her name was to ensure that the people who read her newspaper articles would not know her real name. In her articles, Nellie spoke out against many things in the world that were unfair.

Nellie's first published newspaper article was an angry reply to an opinion written by a columnist in the Pittsburgh newspaper. **(Fold at Fold Line, cut 1 to 2.)** His article said that women should not want to do anything other than stay home with their families or teach. The article said that women were not capable of anything else because they had "inferior brains." After reading this, Nellie was so angry that she wrote a reply back to the editor.

In her letter, Nellie described what it was like to be a woman who wanted and needed to find a job. She wrote about her own frustrating job search. The only jobs that Nellie found open to women offered very low pay, such as factory or kitchen work. Nellie said women could do many jobs that were done by men, and they should get paid the same amount as men for these jobs. She did not sign her name.

The editor of the paper recognized that the letter was very well-written, and he put an ad in the newspaper asking the writer of the letter to come and meet him at his office.

When the editor met Nellie, he was impressed with her and offered her a job as a reporter for five dollars a week. That was about twice what a woman could earn by working in a factory.

Nellie chose to write an article about divorce. **(Cut 3 to 4.)** She called it "Mad Marriages." Back then, divorce was considered to be so awful that no one talked about it. But Nellie believed that everyone needed to know how unfair divorce laws were to women. Nellie wrote that women should be free to choose whom they wanted to marry. If her husband mistreated her, a woman should have the right to get a divorce. Nellie's articles helped sell a lot of newspapers.

Nellie decided that she could help women by writing about their jobs and their lives. She called her articles "Our Workshop Girls." She wrote about how long and hard women worked, and how dangerous some of their jobs were. She wrote about children who were forced to work in horrible factories. When a factory owner would not let her enter their factory to talk to the workers, Nellie disguised herself as a worker in order to get inside. She would work in the factory for several days, then write articles based on her experience. She wrote so well that her articles made the reader feel as if he or she were standing right there in the factory with Nellie. **(Cut from 5 to 6.)**

Nellie didn't just visit factories, she also went to the very poor neighborhoods where the factory workers lived. Her stories led to new laws that helped protect the women and children she wrote about.

By the time she was twenty-one years old, Nellie was the most-loved newspaper reporter in Pittsburgh, loved by her readers that is. She was also the most-hated newspaper reporter in Pittsburgh, hated by the owners of the places about which she wrote.

Needing a new challenge, Nellie volunteered to travel to Mexico and send back articles about America's southern neighbor. **(Cut from 7 to 8.)** Newspaper readers all across the country enjoyed Nellie's articles about the Mexican countryside, the culture and the people of Mexico. Once again, her stories talked about the problems that faced the poor, especially women and children.

On her return to the United States, Nellie moved to New York City because she wanted to be a reporter for a larger newspaper. But no one would hire her because she was a woman. Finally, after refusing to leave the newspaper office of Joseph Pulitzer, Nellie got a job there by promising to write an article about one of the most awful places in the world, the insane asylum on Blackwell's Island. The insane asylum was a hospital for mentally ill patients.

No one except persons who were considered insane and the hospital workers were allowed on Blackwell's Island. The only way Nellie could get in was to pretend she was mentally ill. So Nellie rented a room in a very poor part of town and acted mentally disturbed. A few days later, the landlady called the police. The police took her to a nearby hospital. After several days in the hospital, the doctors declared Nellie severely mentally ill. She was sent to Blackwell's Island. **(Unfold and cut corners of paper from 9 to 10 and 11 to 12. Place asylum over black paper.)**

Now Nellie could find out first-hand what it was like to be a patient in an insane asylum. Just like the other inmates, Nellie ate terrible food, slept on a rickety bed in a cold locked room, and sat on a hard bench all day with nothing to do. As soon as she arrived at the hospital, Nellie began to act perfectly normal and asked to be released. She insisted that she was not mentally ill. But no one paid any attention to her. The doctors and nurses just ignored her requests. She was shocked at how badly the patients were treated by the staff. It was much like a prison. Nellie began to worry that the publisher of the newspaper had forgotten his promise to get her out of the asylum in ten days.

Finally, a lawyer sent by the newspaper arranged for Nellie's release. Nellie immediately began working on her story called "Ten Days in a Madhouse." Her story caused a huge reaction. Thousands of people bought the newspaper just to read her report. Just as Nellie had hoped, conditions improved for the patients at Blackwell's Island. Not only that, asylums all across the country made efforts to improve their care for the mentally ill.

By keeping her promise to write this article, Nellie Bly had earned her job as a reporter for the newspaper. She was the first female reporter hired by Joseph Pulitzer at the New York *World*.

Nellie went on to report unfairness and mistreatment of people in many areas of life. She had a friend accuse her of robbery so that she could learn how police treated accused women in prison. She went to several employment agencies and pretended that she needed a job. Nellie discovered that the agencies charged a fee

before they would help her. Then, after she paid the fee, they recommended her for jobs for which she was clearly not qualified. The agencies also charged a fee to those people who were looking for workers.

Nellie exposed politicians who took bribes. She wrote about how hard it was for a woman to get into law school. After her articles were published, concerned citizens took action to improve the prisons, slums, hospitals and other institutions that she visited.

All this time, the readers of her articles did not know who Nellie Bly really was. Many people were convinced that Nellie was a team of male reporters. They thought that no one person could write so many articles, and certainly not a woman!

In 1889, Nellie began one of the most exciting trips the world has ever known. Before beginning her trip, she let the world know that "Nellie Bly" was a young woman just 26 years of age. Nellie wanted to travel around the world in 80 days, just like the hero in the book *Around the World in Eighty Days* by Jules Verne. Now, it was one thing for a fictional book character to undertake such an adventure, but no one believed that a real person could actually travel around the world in 80 days. People were especially certain that a woman alone could not do it. But Nellie was determined.

Along the way, Nellie sent stories back to New York to be published. Newspaper readers all over the world read about the unusual people, food and sights that Nellie experienced. They read about her delays, her thrill at seeing the American flag in a foreign country, her problems and her triumphs along the way. They marveled that Nellie was traveling all by herself, carrying everything she needed for the trip in one small duffel bag.

Nellie returned to New York in 72 days, six hours and eleven minutes. She had traveled 24,899 miles by train, donkey, handcart and on foot. She had also crossed the oceans of the world on large ships. **(Cut at solid lines 13, 14, 15, 16, and 17. Place on black paper and turn over to show ship.)** With her trip, Nellie Bly had set a new world record. More than that, Nellie had set an example of independence and self-reliance for all the women of the world.

After her trip, Nellie wrote a book about her travels, and continued reporting on problems that needed attention. She wrote an article about people who volunteered their time to help the Salvation Army. After reading this article, many people donated their time and money to this charity. She exposed a well-known mind reader as nothing but a trickster. She interviewed convicted criminals to get their side of the story. In 1894, she traveled to Chicago to write about the violent railroad strike. After thoroughly investigating both sides, she wrote that the strikers did have some real problems, such as poor living conditions, that the company needed to help solve. Nellie also reported on farmers in Nebraska who had suffered two years of terrible summer droughts, and harsh winter blizzards. They were wiped out financially. Nellie helped set up a relief committee to help them through their tough times.

Nellie wrote articles about abandoned children who roamed the streets of New York City. She helped find homes for the children and sometimes even took care of them herself until she could find parents to adopt these children.

Nellie Bly died on January 14, 1922, after a two-week bout with pneumonia. She was 58 years old.

Nellie Bly is often remembered for her amazing trip around the world. Many journalists consider her to be one of the best newspaper reporters in American history. But Nellie was a true heroine because she spent her life reporting on injustices in the hope of helping people who were powerless to help themselves. With her articles, she achieved many social reforms. Nellie Bly was also very effective in proving to herself and the world that a woman can do anything a man can do. Nellie Bly should be remembered for these achievements.

Nellie Bly was only one person, yet through her writing she helped many people.

Activities & Discussion Questions

1. Nellie Bly spent much of her life travelling. As a class, make a list of the different types of transportation available to people of the late 1800s and early 1900s. What types of transportation do we have today that Nellie did not use in her travels? Look up transportation in an encyclopedia to see if you left any out. Consider also looking in the nonfiction section of your library.

2. Nellie Bly was a very famous newspaper reporter. Take a close look at your local newspaper. Locate the following parts of the paper: index, headline, byline, dateline, feature story, advertisement, weather map, sports story, TV section, obituaries, editorial, and comic strip. Cut out and label an example of each one.

3. During Nellie's lifetime, there were many different groups of people who Nellie tried to help with the difficult problems they faced. In today's world, many of the same kinds problems still exist. There are also many organizations that devote their time, energy and money find solutions. Use the Internet to find out more about some of these, including UNICEF, the Red Cross, World Hunger Organization, Toys for Tots, and Goodwill Industries. Are there other organizations that you know about? Share your findings with your class.

4. Nellie Bly was a very good newspaper reporter. What qualities and/or skills do you think made her so good at her job? What would you need to learn to be a reporter for a TV station or newspaper today?

Super Search

Joseph Pulitzer created an award for journalists that is still very important today. What is the name of the award and when was the first one given? Did Nellie ever receive this award? *(Answer: Pulitzer Prizes were first given in 1917. Nellie Bly did not receive one.)*

To learn more about Nellie Bly

Websites

► The American Experience: Around the World in 72 Days.

http://www.pbs.org/wgbh/amex/world/adventure.html

Information on the PBS television program on Nellie Bly, with a teacher's guide. From the Public Broadcasting System and WGBH.

► Books and Biographies: Nellie Bly

http://home.att.net/~gapehenry/BlyBooks.html

A partially annotated list of adult and children's books and websites about Nellie Bly.

► Women's History Project—Nellie Bly

http://www.ozemail.com.au/~mghslib/projects/stwh01.html

A brief biographical sketch. From Macarthur Girls High School (Parramatta, Australia).

Books

Billings, Henry, and Melissa Billings. *Heroes: 21 True Stories of Courage and Honor*. Jamestown, 1985.

Blos, Joan W. *Nellie Bly's Monkey: His Remarkable Story in His Own Words*. Morrow, 1996. Illustrated by Catherine Stock. On her trip around the world, fearless reporter Nellie Bly finds a monkey named McGinty, who accompanies her for the balance of the trip. Easy reading.

Carlson, Judy, and Mike Eagle. *Nothing Is Impossible, Said Nellie Bly*. (Real Readers). Raintree, 1990. Recommended for K–3.

Emerson, Kathy Lee. *Making Headlines: A Biography of Nellie Bly*. Dillion Press, 1989.

Johnston, Johanna. *They Led the Way*. Scholastic, 1973. Stories of fourteen American women.

Quackenbush, Robert. *Stop the Presses, Nellie's Got a Scoop*. Simon & Schuster, 1992.

Peck, Ira., ed. *Nellie Bly's Book: Around the World in 72 Days*. Twenty-first Century, 1999. This is Nellie Bly's own account, edited by Ira Peck.

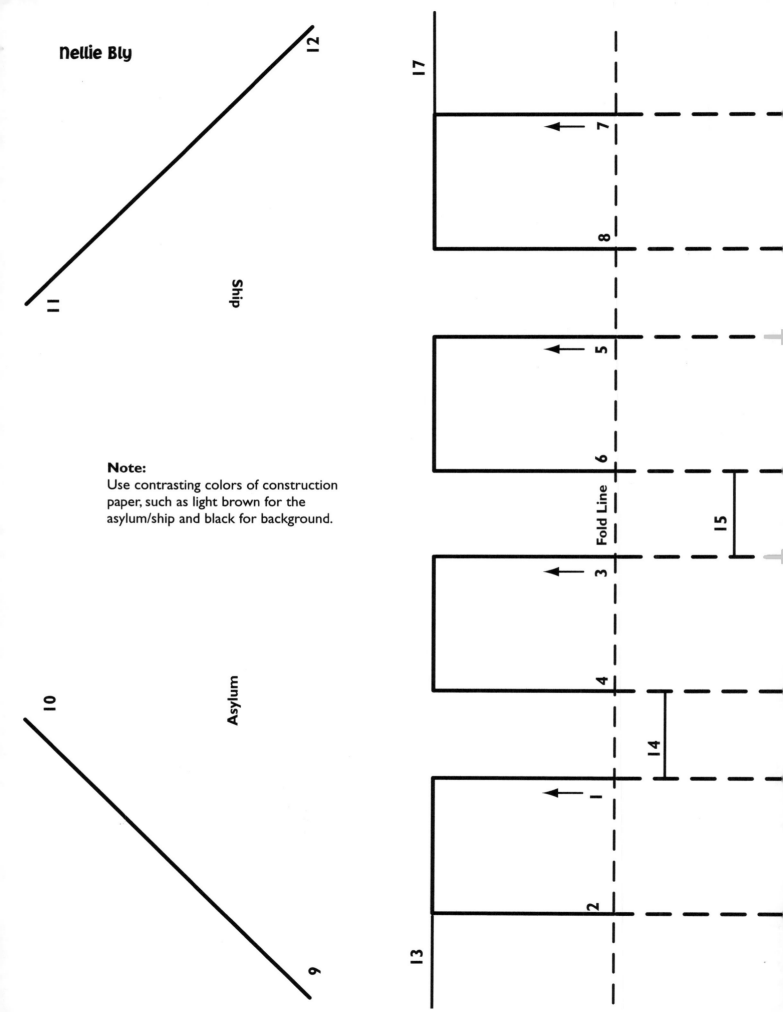

Nellie Bly

Ship

11

12

Note:
Use contrasting colors of construction paper, such as light brown for the asylum/ship and black for background.

Asylum

10

9

Fold Line

17

7

8

5

6

15

3

4

14

1

2

13

Louis Braille

Louis Braille was a boy who desperately wanted to read, but he could not. It was not because he wasn't smart enough or didn't have good teachers. Louis could not read because he was blind. In the early 1800s, there was no way for blind people like Louis to read. So Louis set out to solve this problem for himself and for all blind people.

Here's the story:

Louis was the youngest of five children. His family lived in a farmhouse outside of Paris, France. He was a happy little boy who loved watching his father work. His father was a harness maker. He made bridles, harnesses, and saddles out of leather. His father had a wonderful tool bench filled with all kinds of exciting tools. Some of them were curved **(Draw from 1 to 2, top line of book.)** Some of them were straight **(Draw from 2 to 3, spine of book.)** Some of the tools had very, very sharp blades. **(Draw from 3 to 4 to 5 to 6, blade and bottom of book.)** But all of them were very, very dangerous, especially for a little three-year-old boy who was very, very curious.

Louis's father had warned him many times never to touch the dangerous tools. But one day, Louis disobeyed the rule and went into his father's workshop. He picked up a sharp awl, which is a long pointed tool used for making holes in leather. He pretended to be making a saddle, but the awl slipped and went straight into little Louis's eye! **(Draw from 1 to 4, line down.)** He screamed and everyone came running.

The doctor was sent for and did everything he knew how to do, but Louis' eye soon became infected. Even worse, the infection spread to his other eye. In 1811, the wonderful medicines that we have today were not available. There was nothing anyone could do to help Louis. Three-year-old Louis would be blind for the rest of his life.

Being blind was a terrible handicap for Louis. However, his parents did everything they could to help him become as independent as possible. He had chores to do at home and in his father's workshop. He helped his father by polishing the leather. He rubbed a soft cloth back and forth on the leather until it was smooth. **(Draw line 6 to 7 to 8 to 3, in a back and forth motion.)**

His father carved a long cane for Louis. He could swing it back and forth in front of himself as he walked. That way he would not bump into anything. **(Draw from 9 to 8 to 7 to 10.)** Today, blind people use similar canes to help them get around. Perhaps you have seen a blind person using one of these special white canes with a red tip on the end.

When Louis was six years old, the village priest invited Louis to come to the church a few mornings a week for lessons. Louis did so well at his lessons that the priest arranged for Louis to go to the local school. Children went to school six days a week from eight in the morning until five at night. It was a long day but Louis loved it. He tried to do everything the other children did. But he had to remember everything that was said because he could not read it in a book or write down any notes. **(Draw 2 to 9 to 10, top of book.)** He even did the math problems in his head.

When Louis was ten, his parents sent him to a special school for the blind in Paris. At first Louis was homesick, but he gradually made new friends and got used to the teachers at the school. He was very happy when he discovered he had a great talent for playing the organ and piano.

At the school, there were books with raised letters that a blind reader could feel with his fingertips. But many of the letters were so similar that it took time to read even one word. Each book that used these letters was made by hand, so they were very expensive. The books were also big and hard to store. **(Point out drawing of book.)**

Louis knew that there had to be a better way. But what? People had tried for many years to develop an inexpensive and easy way for blind people to read. No one had succeeded. Reading was so important to Louis, that he decided to devote his energies to this problem.

In 1821, Captain Charles Barbier, a French army captain, came to Paris to visit the school for the blind. He had developed a system of raised dots and dashes to represent words that soldiers could read in the dark with their fingertips. Captain Barbier thought that blind people might be able to use it too. Louis was excited about this reading system, but when he tried it, he discovered that there were many problems. So he set about trying to improve this "point writing" system.

Finally, after working on it in all of his spare time for three years, Louis developed a simple, yet brilliant idea. On a heavy piece of paper he drew a six dot pattern like this: **(On left side of "book," draw six circles.)** Each dot had a number. **(Number the dots one through six.)** Then he used a sharp, pointed instrument to make a raised dot in one of the circles. This was the letter A. **(Color in circle number one and write the letter A.)**

Two raised dots represented the letter B. **(On the right side of "book," draw six circles. Color in circles one and four.)** The first ten letters of the alphabet, letters A through J, use the top four dots. In the next ten letters of the alphabet, letters K through T, the lower left-hand dot is always used. For letters U through Z, the lower right-hand dot and the lower left-hand dot are always used. **(Point to dots as you discuss them.)**

There are 63 possible arrangements of the dots, so there are plenty of combinations to represent the letters of the alphabet, as well as numerals and punctuation marks.

Louis Braille was now fifteen years old, and it had taken him three years of hard work to come up with a reading system that worked well for blind people. Unfortunately, this was not the end of his struggles. His problems were really just beginning.

At first, Louis's method was not accepted—it was rejected! People were unwilling to take an interest in something so different. Furthermore, they did not think that a boy could invent something so important! They asked, "What is wrong with the old method?" Many people back then thought that blind people were not as smart as other people, and they didn't really need to read books.

There was another problem. Money was needed to make new books using Louis' method. But people did not want to give money to make books using a method that was invented by a fifteen-year-old boy.

When Louis was nineteen, he was hired as a teacher in the school. He was a kind, patient teacher who always had time for his students even when he was tired from a long day's work. Often, he would stay up late at night making his raised dot books for the school's library.

He spent several hours a day practicing on the organ, and in 1833 he was appointed organist at one of the biggest churches in Paris. People said that if he would spend his time on his music and forget about those silly raised dot books of his, that he could be a famous organist.

When Louis was 26 years old, he became very ill with tuberculosis. Today there are medicines to treat this disease, but back then, all Louis could do was rest, eat good food and get plenty of fresh air. He decided that even though he was ill, he would continue to fight to get his reading method accepted. He knew that blind people all over the world wanted to read. But for many years, it seemed to Louis that his reading method would never be accepted or used anywhere except at his own school.

But gradually, more and more people began to learn of this easy reading method for the blind. Other teachers in other schools for the blind were willing to give it a try.

In 1847, a braille printing press was made so that pages could be printed much faster and easier. This increased the availability of books for the blind, and it made Louis very happy.

But his health declined, and he did not have the energy to teach, play the organ, or make his braille books. Despite his limited time, Louis did what he could to help others. Finally, in 1852, when he was only 36 years old, Louis died.

It seemed that no one but a few family friends, fellow teachers, and students mourned Louis Braille's death. As time passed, more and more blind people were teaching and using the braille method. Six years after his death, the first American school for the blind used the braille method of reading. Within 30 years, most schools for the blind were teaching with the braille method of reading and writing.

One hundred years after his death, Louis's coffin was taken from his home town and moved to Paris to be reburied next to France's most honored men and women. Many people attended the event to celebrate and remember Louis and his simple life of teaching.

Louis Braille was one man with a disability. As a result of his handicap, he spent his life helping others.

Thanks to Louis Braille's invention, blind people all over the world are able to read for information and enjoyment, enabling them to do all the things he imagined for them. **(Point to drawing again.)**

Activities & Discussion Questions

1. Using the braille alphabet you find at the General Braille website (http://disdev.stu.umn.edu/AltForm/brail-guide.html), select a word from the story and write it in braille. To make the raised dots, use the end of a paintbrush or ball point pen on heavy paper. When you're finished, exchange papers with someone and "translate" the dots using the braille website.

2. With his invention, Louis Braille changed the world for blind people. Can you name other inventions that help people who are handicapped in other ways? If you could invent one new thing that would help handicapped people, what would it be and why?

3. Despite his handicap, Louis Braille invented a way to read and write. Using one of the websites suggested, learn more about the special machines and computer adaptations that are available today to blind people. Write a paragraph about one of these.

4. When Louis Braille was alive, blind people were considered of inferior intelligence and often led lives of poverty and despair. Discuss how blind people are treated today. If one of your fellow classmates had poor eyesight, how could you and your classmates help him or her?

Super Search Question

What is Web-Braille? How does it work? Use this Library of Congress site as a resource (http://www.loc.gov/nls/nls-wb.html).

To learn more about Louis Braille

Websites

► International Braille Research Center
http://www.braille.org

This site provides a short overview of Braille and the International Braille Research Center.

► Louis Braille
http://www.duxburysystems.com/braille.html
Information about Louis Braille and the early Braille translators and embossers, as well as links to other sites can be found on this website. From Joseph E. Sullivan, Duxbury Systems, Inc.

► Louis Braille Center
http://www.louisbraillecenter.org
This website lists books in Braille and lesson plans available for purchase for grades four through eight. From the Louis Braille Center.

► New York Institute for Special Education. Blindness Resource Center
http://www.Nyise.org/braille.htm
The New York Institute for Special Education includes an in-depth history of the first school for the blind, Louis Braille, and links to many other resources.

Books

Adler, David. *A Picture Book of Louis Braille*. Holiday House, 1997. This is a biography for younger children.

Brill, Marlene Targ. *Extraordinary Young People*. Children's Press, 1996. This book contains stories about the remarkable achievements of children and young adults.

Bryant, Jennifer Bryant. *Louis Braille: Inventor*. Chelsea House, 1994. This is an informative biography with appropriate historical background.

Davidson, Margaret. *Louis Braille: The Boy Who Invented Books for the Blind*. Scholastic, 1971. This includes a diagram of the Braille alphabet for primary readers.

Fradin, Dennis. *Louis Braille: The Blind Boy Who Wanted to Read*. Silver Burdett, 1997. The author uses a straightforward style with full-page period paintings for grades two to four.

Louis Braille

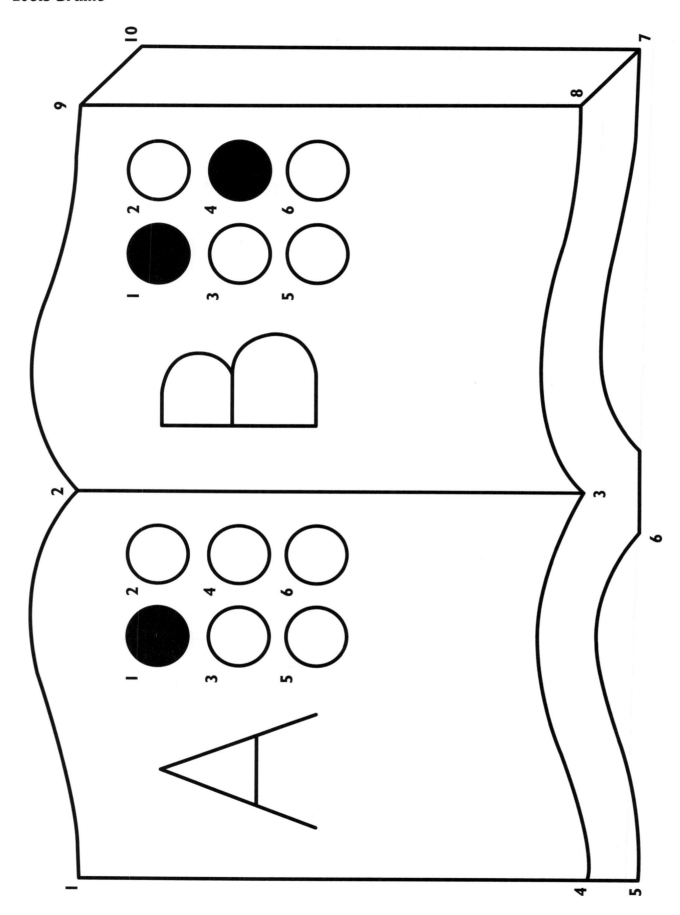

Andrew Carnegie

Do you like to come to the library and borrow books? Yes, of course you do. Libraries are an important part of our lives. It is really great that you can get all the books and information that you want from the library. And it is free. **(1. Draw one book on each side of page.)**

Let's name some other wonderful things that we enjoy:

Have you ever listened to beautiful organ music? It can make you feel good about yourself and the world. All across America, there are organs in churches of all faiths. Over 8,000 of these churches received their organs as a gift. **(2. Draw organ with pipes.)**

Medical research laboratories cost millions of dollars to build and run. Researchers need buildings and equipment in order to look for new ways to help sick people.

We need to learn more about the ocean; how can we use it properly, and how it can help us. Special equipment and research specialists are needed to study the oceans. Again, these things cost lots of money.

In 1919, a 100-inch optical telescope and observatory was built in California with donated money. It doubled our knowledge of the universe. **(3. Draw telescope/observatory.)**

People can learn many things by going to an art gallery, a museum, or a program given in a concert hall.

All of these things involve learning. But what else do they have in common? They were all made possible with money given by a man named Andrew Carnegie. He was an extremely rich man who made most of his money from selling the steel made in his Pennsylvania steel mills.

Andrew Carnegie emigrated from Scotland in 1847, when he was twelve years old. His family came to America in order to make a better life for themselves. They moved to Pittsburgh, Pennsylvania, because several of their relatives had immigrated there. Andrew's father wove cloth on a hand loom and his mother sewed shoes.

Andrew worked in several different factories as a young boy. When he was seventeen, he went to work for the railroad. He worked his way up in the company, and he invested the extra money that he earned in an oil company, a bridge company, an iron mill, and a company that made railroad cars. These were all good investments, and Andrew was on his way to making even more money.

All of his companies made products that needed iron. But iron wore out very quickly under heavy use, such as in railroad tracks. Steel contains iron, but steel also contains other metals to make it stronger. So Mr. Carnegie began making and selling steel from the steel mills he owned. **(4. Draw steel mill and smoke.)**

This was a time when America was building many new factories, office buildings and bridges. Steel was in great demand for all these projects, and Andrew Carnegie was a good salesman for his steel mills. His companies were very profitable.

Andrew Carnegie's steel was used to build the Washington Monument which was finished in 1884. This special building gave Carnegie great pride, because George Washington had been one of his heroes since he was a young boy.

At age 65, Andrew Carnegie set out to do something that he later described as being harder than earning his money, and that was wisely giving his money away.

Andrew Carnegie was an accomplished writer, and had written articles and books over the years that were read by many people. In his articles, he explained his belief that gift money should be used to help people help themselves. He was convinced that ignorance was the country's biggest enemy. He said that the minds of our citizens represent our country's greatest wealth. Carnegie reasoned that if people became more knowledgeable, then many of the world's problems could be solved. This is why he gave his money to colleges, museums, libraries, and scientific research laboratories.

He said that money should not be given directly to the poor. Instead, he wanted the money that he donated to be used to help prevent the problems that caused poverty. He gave money to build new schools. People could go to these schools to learn new job skills.

He also gave money to help teachers learn how to become better teachers. He established a pension, or old-age fund just for teachers, because he believed that teachers were underpaid.

Carnegie thought that if there was a way to help countries deal with international problems, the problems might not develop into wars. So he set up an organization called the Endowment for International Peace. This group works to promote peace throughout the world.

Carnegie's favorite endowment was his worldwide Hero Fund Commission. This organization gives rewards for bravery to ordinary individuals or their surviving dependents. Carnegie was thinking of the families of heroes who gave their lives to save others.

By the time he died in 1919, Andrew Carnegie had donated 350 million dollars to thousands of libraries and institutions of learning. In giving away his money, he established a new way for wealthy people to distribute their wealth so that the greatest number of people might benefit from it. He set up the Carnegie Corporation, which is in charge of distributing his money to this day. This type of giving later became known as a foundation. With his foundation, Carnegie set an example that other wealthy people in America and other countries have followed.

After Andrew Carnegie retired, he remained very busy. But he also enjoyed looking back over his life and remembering all of the many different places in the world that he visited. One of his favorite trips was the one he took with his mother in 1881. They traveled back to Andrew's childhood home in Scotland. The entire town turned out to welcome them. **(5. Draw line.)**

It was here that Andrew gave money for a special building. He was later to give money to any town in America that wanted one of these buildings. The town only had to promise to continue to support the building with tax funds after it was built. Does anyone know what kind of building this was? Yes, a library. **(Fold at lines A and B, then show library.)**

It all started with the library that he gave to his home town in Scotland. This library began what was to be an important program for Carnegie-founding libraries. He considered libraries to be among the most important buildings in every community. Many towns recognized the importance of their library by inscribing "Open to All" or "Let There Be Light" over the door. **(Write "Let There Be Light" over the door.)**

Andrew Carnegie came to America with no money and few skills. Through hard work, determination, a little bit of luck, and the opportunity that America provided for him, he became one of the world's richest men. By the time of his death, he had donated over 80 percent of his wealth, and millions of people in the world have benefited from his gifts.

Andrew Carnegie was just one person, but he made a difference in everyone's life.

Activities & Discussion Questions

1. Why do you think Carnegie believed libraries were so important? Did Andrew Carnegie give money to build a library in your town? How could you find out? If your town did have a Carnegie library, is the building still being used for a library? Has the library been remodeled?

2. Can you think of any other persons who have donated large amounts of money for worthy causes? Can you recall any recent donations? Where would you look for this type of information?

3. Andrew Carnegie gave his money to help make people's lives better in many areas. Imagine that you have just been given one million dollars by a relative. One of the conditions of the gift is that you have to give it all away to benefit your community. Discuss how you would spend this money. How might you decide whether the donations were used wisely?

4. Dunfermline, Scotland, was the birthplace of Carnegie. Locate this town on a map, globe, or atlas. How many miles did Andrew and his family travel when they immigrated from their hometown to their new home in Pittsburgh, Pennsylvania? Can you use the map's distance scale to determine this distance?

Super Search Question

Try some of the websites listed in the resource list to determine how many Carnegie libraries were constructed. Hint: Try Philanthropy 101 on the PBS site. *(Answer: 2,811 libraries throughout the English-speaking world)*

To learn more about Andrew Carnegie

Websites

► Carnegie and His Philanthropies
http://www.carnegie.org/
Brief biographical information and links to other Carnegie institutions.

► The Entrepreneur's Hall of Fame: Andrew Carnegie.
http://www.ltbn.com/tribcarnegie.html
Provides information on Carnegie's life and accomplishments from a business perspective. From Let's Talk Business Network, Inc.

► Meet Andrew Carnegie
http://www.pbs.org/wgbh/pages/amex/carnegie/meet.html
From the *American Experience* television series. Provides insight into Carnegie's philosophy and time, with teacher resources. From the Public Broadcasting System.

Books

Bowman, John. *Andrew Carnegie: Steel Tycoon.* Silver Burdett, 1989.

Jones, Theodore. *Andrew Carnegie Libraries Across America: A Public Legacy.* John Wiley, 1997. 192 pp. This comprehensive look at the story of Andrew Carnegie and at the libraries he built. Includes pictures representing the different architectural styles.

Simon, Charnan. *Andrew Carnegie: Builder of Libraries.* (Community Builders) Children's Press, 1998. This book describes the efforts of Carnegie to build public libraries as a way of improving community life in Pittsburgh and other places.

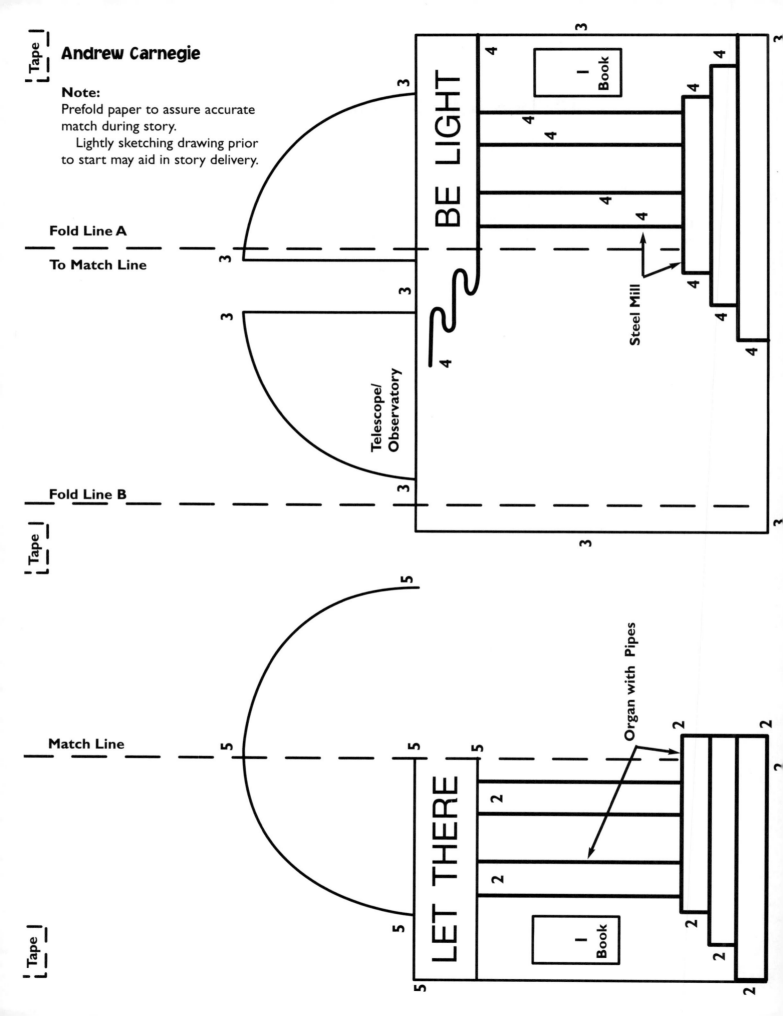

Roberto Clemente

"Roberto was born to play baseball," said Roberto's mother, Luisa. Roberto was born over 60 years ago on the island of Puerto Rico. **(1. Draw circle for island, baseball.)** There were seven children in his family and his father worked for a sugarcane company. Cutting sugar cane with a four foot long, razor-sharp machete was hard, dangerous work. It was also hot and dirty work.

When Roberto and his friends were little, they loved to play baseball, but they did not have enough money to buy real baseballs. That did not stop Roberto. He made his own baseballs by wrapping string around old golf balls. **(2. Draw second circle and lines across circle.)** To hold the string in place, he wrapped tape around the ball. **(3. Draw line in first circle, baseball seam.)**

Roberto and his friends spent hours playing baseball, talking about baseball, and listening to baseball games on the radio. While they were walking to school, Roberto and his friends threw rubber balls back and forth. Roberto always had a rubber ball in his hands. He squeezed it continually to strengthen his fingers and wrists.

Roberto learned the value of education and self-discipline from his parents. When he was nine years old, Roberto wanted a bicycle. His father told him that he would have to earn it. So Roberto delivered milk each morning before school. He saved his earnings for three years to buy a used bicycle that cost $27. How old do you think Roberto was before he had his own bicycle? (twelve years old) How old were you when you got a bicycle? **(4. Draw line for bicycle frame.)**

As soon as Roberto entered high school, he excelled in many sports. He was on both the track and the baseball teams. One day Roberto played baseball with the Crabbers, a winter team in Puerto Rico. The owner of the team saw Roberto and hired him to play. So in 1952, at the age of eighteen, Roberto became a professional baseball player.

In the spring of 1954, Roberto signed a contract with the Brooklyn Dodgers. Then he was drafted from the Brooklyn team to the Pittsburgh Pirates in November of 1954. Roberto later said, "I didn't even know where Pittsburgh was."

At first, Roberto found life difficult in the United States because of language and cultural barriers. He became angry when his teammates teased him because he did not understand their jokes. But over time Roberto learned more about life in the U.S. and how to get along with his teammates.

The Pittsburgh Pirates became a better team after Roberto joined. Roberto played right field. He was also skilled at batting, throwing, and catching fly balls. In 1966, Roberto became the first Puerto Rican to win the Most Valuable Player (MVP) Award. This award is voted on by sports writers. Roberto was pleased with this honor, but he was also happy because it would have a positive impact on the young people in Puerto Rico. He knew that kids needed "someone to look to and to follow."

When Roberto returned home to Puerto Rico, he was the greatest sports hero in all of Latin America. Throughout his baseball career, Clemente remembered his Puerto Rican heritage and tried to help those who were not as fortunate as he was. He devoted hours of his time to instructing young, aspiring baseball players. He even planned a sports facility for children in Puerto Rico.

In 1970, Roberto was honored at Three Rivers Stadium in Pittsburgh with a Roberto Clemente Night. Many people came all the way from Puerto Rico to see him. He received $6,000, which he donated to the Children's Hospital in Pittsburgh.

On September 30, 1972, Roberto had successfully hit the ball 2,999 times. The world was waiting for his next hit, his number 3,000! And it came! Roberto hit a fastball deep into left center field for a double. The pitcher graciously refused to take the mound in order to give the umpire time to present Clemente with the baseball which he had just hit. The fans cheered wildly. In 103 years of major league baseball, only ten other men had ever hit 3,000! **(5. Draw 3000.)**

On that September night, the world didn't know that Roberto's hit number 3,000 was also to be his very last.

In November, Roberto traveled to Nicaragua with his amateur baseball team. He was the volunteer manager, and they were playing a tournament in Managua, the capital city. While Roberto was there, he met a fourteen-year-old orphan named Julio who had lost both legs in an accident. Roberto arranged to get Julio a pair of artificial legs.

The baseball tournament ended and Roberto returned home on December 6 to be with his wife, three young sons, his parents and other family members.

But on December 23, only two weeks after arriving home, a severe earthquake destroyed much of Managua, Nicaragua. Six thousand people were killed and 20,000 were injured. Many people in the city were left homeless.

Just as he had devoted himself to baseball, Roberto committed himself to helping the earthquake victims. Roberto volunteered to serve as chairman of the Puerto Rican chapter of the Nicaraguan relief effort. He worked tirelessly to persuade friends and strangers to donate whatever they could to help the people of Managua. He went on television and radio to ask for help. He organized a ship to take supplies to Nicaragua. He arranged for three air flights to take vital medical supplies. Roberto spent all of his Christmas helping the earthquake victims.

On December 31, rescue workers requested more medical supplies, a water pump, and an X-ray machine. Roberto decided to take the supplies himself. He had two reasons for going even though his friends and family urged him to stay home and rest. Roberto wanted to see if the orphan Julio was safe. He also wanted to make sure that the supplies got to the people who really needed them.

The only plane available to take them was a rather rickety DC-7 cargo plane. The flight was delayed repeatedly by mechanical problems. Finally they took off shortly after 9 p.m. on New Year's Eve.

Less than twenty minutes later, the plane crashed in the Atlantic Ocean about one mile offshore. **(6. Draw plane path, thumb of glove.)** Roberto's body was never recovered.

On January 1, 1973, thousands of Puerto Ricans gathered silently on the beach where Roberto's plane had gone down. **(Draw beach, pocket of glove.)** They tossed flowers into the ocean waves. **(Draw waves, fingers of glove.)** Their hero was dead.

Roberto was gone, but his memory was honored in many ways. He was voted the honor of immediate induction into the Baseball Hall of Fame, becoming the first Hispanic to gain recognition in this institution. The Pittsburgh Pirates retired his uniform number, which was number 21. He was the second baseball player to be honored on a United States postage stamp. As one of baseball's all-time great players, Roberto had also received the coveted Golden Glove Award. **(Fold to reveal baseball glove.)**

But more important than all of these baseball honors, people all over the world remembered Roberto's fierce dedication to everything he did; earning money as a kid to buy a used bicycle, becoming a baseball player, helping children participate in sports, and delivering medical supplies to earthquake victims.

Roberto Clemente started out as one youngster who was too poor to even buy a baseball, but through his achievements he inspired and helped thousands of people in need.

Activities & Discussion Questions

1. Here's a riddle: Why do spiders make good baseball players? (*Answer: Because baseball players are so good at catching flies.*) To try some more baseball riddles go to   They should locate (http://www.drblank. com/basrid.htm#10Riddles). If you enjoy these, try looking for riddle books in your school library.

2. Baseball is a sport that many people enjoy playing and watching. But how did it get started? Can you suggest some reference materials in your library to learn about the history of baseball?

3. When the city of Managua, Nicaragua, suffered extensive damage from a big earthquake, Clemente devoted himself to helping the victims. Where can you go to learn more about earthquakes? Discuss this and get different opinions about the best resources on this topic.

4. Roberto Clemente grew up speaking Spanish and later on learned to speak English. Some of the first words he would have needed were baseball terms. Take some of the words from the story and look them up in an English/Spanish dictionary from the library. (In many instances the terms will be the same in both languages.)

Super Search Question

Roberto Clemente was born in Puerto Rico and then moved to the United States. What relationship exists between Puerto Rico and the U.S. What type of government does Puerto Rico have? (*Answer: The Puerto Rican people voted to become a commonwealth of the U.S. in 1952. In many ways this is like being one of the states, but there are important differences. One is that Puerto Ricans cannot vote in national elections. This status may change in the future. Source: World Almanac.*)

To learn more about Roberto Clemente
Websites
► Official Roberto Clemente Website
http://www.robertoclemente21.com/
Biographical information, the Roberto Clemente Foundation newsletter, and everything you need to know about the subject, including biographies, links to other sites, and family photos.

► Roberto Clemente
http:www.myhero.com/directory/index.html
Select "Sports" and then Roberto Clemente. Or learn more about one other the other heroes honored on this site. Students may want to contribute their thoughts about their own heroes and heroines.

► Total Baseball Online
http://www.totalbaseball.com/
Select "Players" from the heading across the top of the page. Select "Biographies" to see a list of famous players, including Roberto Clemente.

► Roberto Clemente: A form of punishment
http://www.pirateball.com/glorydays/featuresROBERTO CLEMENTE.html
A biographical account of Clemente's career with the Pittsburgh Pirates.

Books/CD-ROM
Billings, Henry and Melissa Billings. *Heroes: 21 True Stories of Courage and Honor.* Jamestown, 1985.

Bjarkman, Peter C. *Roberto Clemente.* Chelsea House, 1991.

Gilbert, Thomas. *Roberto Clemente.* Chelsea House, 1991.

Greene, Carol. *Roberto Clemente.* Children's Press, 1991.

Macht, Norm L. and Bruce Conord. *Roberto Clemente.* (Junior World Biographies) Chelsea House, 1994.

"Roberto Clemente." *Microsoft Encarta.* Microsoft, 1998. CD-ROM.

West, Alan. *Roberto Clemente: Baseball Legend.* (Hispanic Heritage) Millbrook Press, 1994. Early elementary reading level.

Roberto Clemente

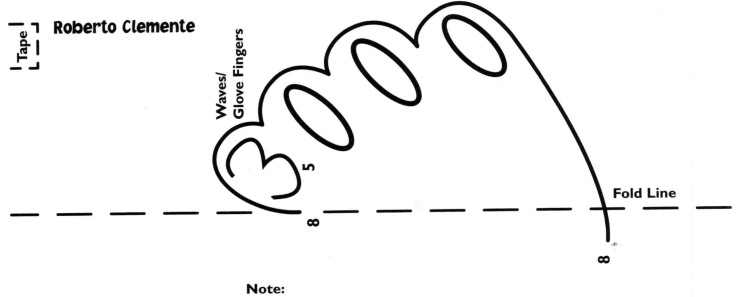

Waves/
Glove Fingers

5

8

Fold Line

8

Note:
Draw on larger paper for best group presentation.

    Prefold paper and lightly presketch drawing to aid presentation delivery.

Fold Line

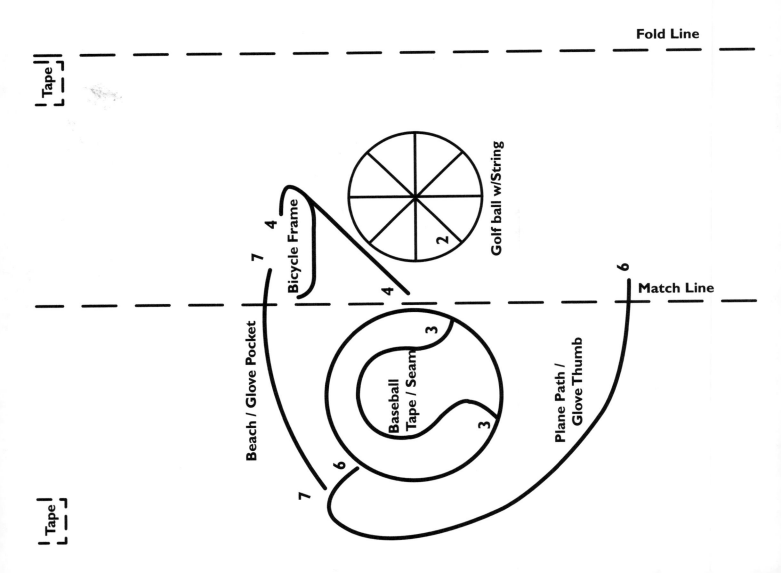

Golf ball w/String

2

Bicycle Frame

4

7

4

Beach / Glove Pocket

3

Baseball
Tape / Seam

3

6

Match Line

Plane Path /
Glove Thumb

6

7

Walt Disney

Walt Disney was born in 1901, and his cartoons, television programs, movies, books, music, vacation spots and nature films continue to affect our lives in a wonderful way. The characters he created are known all over the world, and they have brought fun to millions of people. **(Fold at line A. Cut from 1 to 2.)**

I bet that you all have seen lots of Disney movies, haven't you? Raise your hand if you have ever been to Disney World or Disneyland. They are really fun places to go, aren't they? Have you ever had a mouse lunch box, T-shirt, or a mouse hat with ears on it? How many ears does a mouse have? That's right, two ears. **(Cut from 3 to 4, then show mouse ears.)**

Walt Disney had a gift for creating fun for everyone. He knew that most people work very hard every day at school, at home, and at work. So Disney worked hard to give people a little break from their work. Disney believed that everyone needed to have some fun and fantasy in their lives. **(Unfold paper.)**

Disney started out life in Chicago. He had three brothers and one sister. His father was a carpenter and his mother drew the construction plans for the houses that Walt's father built. **(Fold at line B.)**

Later, the family moved to Missouri where his father had a farm for six years. **(Cut out at line 5.)** During that time, Walt enjoyed watching and painting the farm animals. Here is Walt's paint brush. **(Show paint brush.)** Then his father sold the farm and the family moved to Kansas City where Walt and his father had a very large paper route. While he was living in Kansas City, he studied drawing and cartooning.

When Walt Disney was sixteen, our country became involved in World War I. Walt wanted to help but he was too young to join the army. So he became an ambulance driver in France. He was there for almost a year.

When he returned home, he told his father that he wanted to make his living by being an artist. He got a job in Kansas City drawing and painting cartoons that were used in advertisements. The advertisements were shown before a feature movie in movie theaters.

Walt Disney opened his first studio in an old garage in Hollywood, California. There, he and his brother Roy drew an animated film about a mouse named Mickey. This was one of the very first films that had a soundtrack or sounds to go with the actions of the characters. It was successful and Disney was able to move out of the garage and into a bigger studio. Walt and Roy made more cartoon movies after that and hired other artists to help them.

Before making a cartoon or movie, Walt Disney would gather all his artists together and tell them the story that he wanted them to draw. Walt was a great storyteller, and he acted out all the parts as he told the story. For the story of *Snow White*, he acted out each dwarf. With Walt's acting ability, each dwarf seemed to come alive, and each dwarf had his very own personality. After that, everyone was anxious to begin drawing and painting *Snow White and the Seven Dwarfs*. This was the first full-length cartoon and it was made in 1937.

During World War II, Walt Disney helped our country by making educational films. After the war, he concentrated on films that featured real animals. These films showed how animals lived in nature. The shows also helped people develop an awareness and appreciation of nature.

Walt Disney also made movies featuring people instead of cartoons. Have you ever seen *Mary Poppins*? He hosted a weekly television show which featured many of these stories. *Davy Crockett* was a favorite television show created by Walt Disney. These shows were watched by millions of children and their parents. In all of his shows, movies, and cartoons, Disney presented exceptionally high quality work and used many new techniques that he himself developed. **(Refold at line A and cut from 6 to 7.)**

Walt Disney got the idea to build a theme park while he was taking his own children around to entertainment parks on the weekends. He wanted to build a special place where people of all ages could go to vacation and get away from their everyday world of work. Disneyland opened in 1955 in California.

Walt Disney and the artists who helped him create the movies and shows, received lots of recognition. Walt Disney has won more than 50 Academy Awards, seven Emmys, and 30 Oscars. Walt Disney also received honorary degrees from Yale and Harvard Universities. He died in December, 1966, when he was 65 years old.

In 1971, Walt Disney World opened in Florida. EPCOT, a permanent world's fair dedicated to science and the diversity of the world's cultures, opened next to Disney World in 1982. **(Cut from 8 to 9.)**

Today, millions of people from all over the world enjoy vacations at Disney Theme Parks in the United States, France, and Tokyo. The entire world enjoys Disney movies, games and toys designed or inspired by the creative genius of Walt Disney. He started with a simple cartoon using a mouse that is now recognized all over the world. **(Cut from 10 to 11.)**

In addition to creating all of these memorable things for other people, Walt Disney also supported many charitable causes, such as "Toys for Tots." He also served as an effective representative for the United States in South America for our country's Good Neighbor Policy.

We remember Walt Disney as someone who was committed to families and spent his life providing outstanding family entertainment. He brought joy and laughter to millions of children and adults. Disney added color to our lives through fantasy, and imagination. Today, Disney productions continue to entertain and inspire, through the use of animation and color. **(Fold at line C to show colors through holes. Show paint brush again.)**

Walt Disney used his gift of creativity to build the Disney empire. He said, "Get a good idea and stay with it. Work at it until it's done, and done right."

Walt Disney has inspired us to believe that, "All our dreams can come true—if we have the courage to pursue them."

Activities & Discussion Questions

1. Walt Disney made many movies that showed how animals live in nature. If you could go anywhere in the world to film any animal that you wanted, where would you choose to go and why? How could you find out about that place and the animals that are native to that part of the world?

2. Make a list of all of the Disney movies that you have seen. Now rank them in order of your most favorite to least favorite. Why do you like your favorite movie? Write down two of the characters from your favorite movie. Now find a friend who picked a different favorite movie. Think about the two characters that you picked and the two characters that your friend chose. Combine these four new characters into a new story. Remember to create a story that has a beginning, middle and end.

3. When your parents plan a vacation, they need to estimate the costs. If you were helping them to plan a vacation to Disney World, how could you find out how much it would cost? (Besides travel guides, suggest they try one of the websites below.) Do these resources include all the costs? What more do you need to consider?

4. When he was a young boy, Walt Disney loved to draw. Do you like to draw? Check out some "how to draw" books from your library to get some ideas for drawings you might like to do. But don't just look at the book right-side up. Turn the drawing in the book upside down or sideways. This will give you some new ideas.

Super Search Question

If you were going to do report on Walt Disney's life, you would need research from several different resources. Find and write down at least four specific books, articles or websites that you might use.

To learn more about Walt Disney

Websites

► Walt Disney

http://www.intergraffix.com/walt/nindex.htm

This site offers biographical information about Walt Disney and his films.

► Disney.com

http://disney.go.com/

This is the home page for Disney. Select "Disney A–Z" for a biography of Walt Disney, including photos.

► Walt Disney World

http://disney.go.com/DisneyWorld/index2.html

This is the home page for Walt Disney World with links to information on feature attractions, events, lodging, etc.

Books

Fanning, Jim. *Walt Disney*. Chelsea House, 1994.

Greene, Katherine and Richard. *The Man Behind the Magic: The Story of Walt Disney*. Viking Children's Press, 1998. Biography with photographs. The hardcover edition was selected for 1992 International Reading Association-Children's Book Council Children's Choice Award.

Hammontree, Marie. *Walt Disney: Young Movie Maker*. (Childhood of Famous Americans). Aladdin Paperbacks, 1997. Story of Disney as a farm boy in Missouri.

Schroeder, Russell, ed. *Walt Disney: His Life in Pictures*. Disney Press, 1996.

Selden, Bernice. *The Story of Walt Disney, Maker of Magical Worlds*. Yearling Books, 1989. Biography available in paperback.

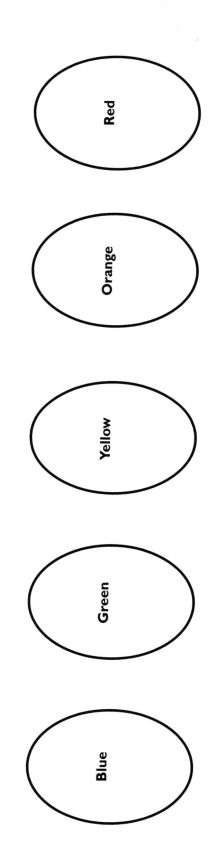

Walt Disney

Note:
Photocopy this page and the previous page onto one sheet as shown below, Prefold at fold lines and color in ovals on back of paper with different colors before telling the story,

Front Side

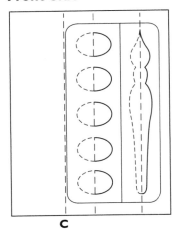

C

Back Side

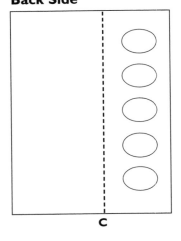

C

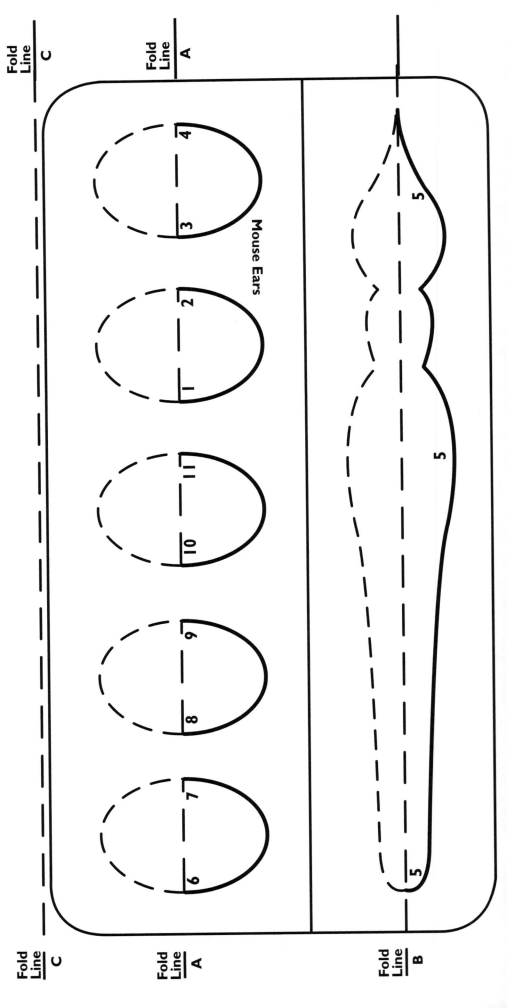

Mouse Ears

Terry Fox

What race is run by 600,000 people around the world? The first time this race was run, only one man ran—and he never crossed the finish line. But even though he never completed the race, he inspired thousands of people all over the world to run and win.

Terry Fox was just an ordinary guy from western Canada who loved to play basketball and hang out with his friends. He was a fine athlete, making the basketball team his freshman year in college. But Terry's right leg kept bothering him so he finally went to the doctor.

The doctor had very bad news for Terry. He said that Terry had bone cancer and his leg had to be amputated, or taken off, six inches above his knee. Terry was heartbroken because he would have to give up his dream of being a professional athlete. Losing his dream was harder than losing his leg. **(Draw leg 1 to 2.)**

While Terry was is the hospital getting treated for his cancer, he saw lots of other cancer patients. They looked tired and scared. Some of them had lost hope. Terry decided that he himself would not lose hope. He also decided that he needed to do something to help other cancer patients. They needed to get their hope back. This would help them feel better.

But what could Terry do? He could barely walk himself, with his new artificial leg and a cane. Then Terry read a magazine article about a man with an artificial leg who had run in the New York Marathon. That gave him a great idea.

Terry decided to run across Canada. He decided to call his run the "Marathon of Hope." This would be a great way to raise money for cancer research. Terry also wanted to prove that cancer victims could still be athletes. He wanted to show the world that he had the courage and desire to help himself and other cancer victims fight this disease in every way possible.

No one took Terry seriously at first. Canada is a huge country. It would be extremely difficult to run across it, even for a person with two healthy legs! Besides, Terry had not even planned to run the shortest route across Canada. He had planned a 5,300 mile route through the most populated areas. **(Draw from 3 to 4.)**

But Terry started writing to companies asking for donations for his run. He got the support of the Canadian Cancer Society. He organized a dance to raise money, and his mother helped him organize garage sales to raise more money. He needed money to buy lots of running shoes, and for food and living expenses along the way.

Terry started training for his run across Canada. At first he ran very short distances. Soon he could run a mile. Now people began to take Terry Fox and his Marathon of Hope Run seriously. In order to improve his strength and for fun, Terry joined a wheelchair basketball team. Soon he could run 25 miles a day. In total, Terry ran 3,000 miles to train for his run across Canada.

On April 12, 1980, he started out in St. John's, Newfoundland. Television crews were there to announce to the nation the start of Terry's run. That morning on TV, he told the world that he was planning to raise at least one million dollars for cancer research. He was planning to run 30 or 40 miles a day in order to finish in six months. He wore jogging shorts so that everyone could see that someone with an artificial leg could still run.

Along the way, friends and strangers invited him into their homes for a meal, an overnight stay or just some time to rest. Everywhere he went he inspired people with his courage and dedication to his cause. Children gave their allowance money for cancer research, and one town of 10,000 people gave $10,000. Terry really wanted to raise one dollar per person in his homeland of Canada.

Terry's run was very difficult at times. Occasionally, trucks passed by Terry too closely and nearly ran him off the road. He ran under the terribly hot summer sun. **(Draw 5, circle.)** He ran through cold weather with blowing rain, snow, and hail. His artificial leg often became loose and he had to stop and fix it the best he could.

Soon after he started running, the Canadian people began to notice Terry. They listened to news stories about his run and how he was doing. They learned the story behind Terry's run across Canada and his goal of one dollar a person donation to cancer research. Soon, everyone was sending in their dollar or more. In one month Terry had raised $100,000.

When Terry ran into a town, crowds gathered along the route and greeted him with cheers. Radio stations played a song called, "Run, Terry, Run." Terry had become a celebrity. Everyone wanted to shake his hand. **(Draw from 3 to 6.)** They wanted to get his autograph and invite him to fund raising dinners.

Terry Fox had inspired the whole country. Soon, other people began doing things to raise money for cancer.

One hundred and forty three days after beginning his run, Terry had run 3,339 miles and raised over $2 million for cancer research.

But on September 1, 1980, Terry experienced sharp pains in his lungs and had to stop running. **(Draw from 6 to 1 and 7 to 2.)** He was taken to the hospital in Thunder Bay, Ontario. There doctors discovered that the cancer had spread to Terry's lungs.

The people of Canada were very disappointed to learn that Terry' could not finish his run. So, less than a week later, a major television network held a telethon for Terry Fox. Major stars danced, sang and asked for money in Terry Fox's name. They raised over ten and one half million dollars in one night!

On September 18, 1980, just eighteen days after ending his run, Terry became the youngest Canadian ever to receive Canada's highest civilian honor, the Companion of the Order of Canada. He was just twenty-two years old. Other honors were given him. A postage stamp was dedicated in his honor and his portrait was hung in Canada's Sports Hall of Fame.

Nine months later, Terry Fox died. Flags across the nation were flown at half-mast and millions watched his funeral on TV. People had donated a total of $25 million toward finding a cure for cancer.

Terry's race was over. But for thousands of others in Canada and around the world, their race was just beginning. September 13 was dedicated as the Terry Fox Marathon of Hope Day. Every year on that day, concerned people all across Canada run, walk or jog six miles to raise money for cancer research. Even people with artificial legs participate, just like Terry Fox. **(Draw from 1 to 8.)** The sixteenth annual Terry Fox Run in September of 1996 set a fund-raising record of $12.5 million. Over 600,000 runners across the world participated.

Terry inspired people to raise money for a good cause. Terry also inspired people with disabilities to have hope and courage in the face of their problems. He was just one ordinary guy with an extraordinary problem. We should salute Terry Fox because he showed the world how to face a challenge—with courage and selfless determination—in order to make things better for others. **(Draw from 7 to 4.)**

Activities & Discussion Questions

1. Where might you locate information about a local run or walk to raise money. *(There are two likely alternatives: Many public libraries and chambers of commerce maintain a local events calendar listing sponsors. Second, many hospitals sponsor a variety of runs or walks in order to raise money for a particular cause.)* Using these suggestions, try to find the following information on a local charity run or walk: What is the name of the run? When is it scheduled? How will the money that is raised be spent? Who sponsors the event? Who can participate? How can someone register for participation?

2. Terry Fox choose to run across Canada in order to raise money to be used to find a cure for cancer. With a friend, make a list of other activities that a person could do in order to raise money. Be creative and think of some unusual or fun ones such as hopping on a pogo stick a certain number of minutes for donations. What is a marathon? Think of some fun ones such as a frisbee or yo-yo or hula hoop marathon.

3. Create a slogan and poster for the event you like the best from you list in number 2.

4. Many famous people like Terry Fox and Jerry Lewis are associated with specific charities. Can you identify any other personalities such as athletes or movie and television stars who support different causes? How could you learn more about these charities and their celebrity supporters?

Super Search Question

Terry Fox's goal was to raise one dollar per person in Canada. In 1980, this meant he needed to raise almost $25 million. How much would he need to raise in Canada today if he wanted to do the same thing? How much would you need to raise in the United States if you wanted to raise one dollar per person? *(Answer: U.S., 273,807,000 [approx. from www.census.gov]; Canada, 31,006,000 [approx. from CIA World Factbook at http://www.odci.gov/cia/publications/factbook/ca.html])*

To learn more about Terry Fox

Websites

► Terry Fox Run
http://www.terryfoxrun.org
The official Terry Fox website, includes how to organize runs. From the Terry Fox Foundation.

► Terry Fox
http://myhero.com/ANGELS
A short biography of Terry Fox.

Books

Billings, Henry, and Melissa Billings. *Heroes: Twenty-one True Stories of Courage and Honor.* Jamestown, 1985.

Brown, Jeremy, and Gail Harvey. *Terry Fox.* General Publishing, 1980.

Scrivener, Leslie. *Terry Fox: His Story.* McClelland and Stewart, 1983.

Zola, Meguida. *Terry Fox.* Grolier, 1984.

For more information on Terry Fox or the foundation, write to:
  Darrell Fox, National Director
  Terry Fox Foundation
  60 St. Clair Ave. E, Ste. 605,
  Toronto, Ontario,
  Canada

Terry Fox

Florence Kelley

1 Raise your hand if your mother makes you do work at home.

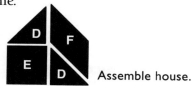

Assemble house.

What work, or chores do you have to do? How long does it take you? If you had to clean up your kitchen, take out the trash, do your homework, sort the laundry, mow the lawn, feed your dog, and clean your room all in one day, you might think that you were overworked!

2 But no, compared with some children in the early 1800s, your chores are very easy. Some children worked in factories and had very tiring and difficult lives. The children came from families who were poor. Their parents could not get jobs that paid them enough money to buy food and clothes so the children also had to work.

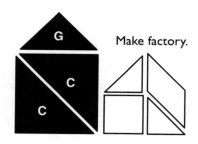

Make factory.

These children were hired by factory owners to work long hours at machines that wove cotton cloth or other products. The machines were easy to operate, so easy in fact that children could run the machines. The factory owners liked hiring children to work in their factories because they did not have to pay children as much money as they had to pay their adult workers.

Let's discuss what a typical day might have been like for a child who worked in a cotton mill. At 5:00 a.m. in the morning darkness, a loud piercing factory whistle blew to wake up the town. The children got up quickly, splashed cold water

on their faces, dressed, and ran from where they lived to the factory. At 6:00 a.m., the factory whistle blew again. This meant that everyone had to be in the factory ready to start work. The factory doors were shut. If any child was late, even by just one minute, they were not paid for their first hour of work.

3 What type of work did children do in factories? In cotton mills, children worked at looms that wove cloth.

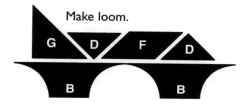

Make loom.

Some boys worked changing the bobbins of thread in a loom. When one bobbin was empty, the bobbin boy had to climb up onto the machine and replace it with a new one. This was very dangerous because the bobbin boy could slip and fall into the machine.

Girls greased the machines and tied broken threads together. But if a lock of their hair or the sleeve of their dress got caught in the machine, they could get badly hurt.

And then there was the noise. The factories were terribly loud because so many large machines were running all at once. The factories were also poorly lit, dirty, smelly and cold.

4 In glass factories, small children had to carry boxes of newly made glass bottles.

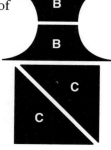

Make glass bottle.

The bottles were hot because they had just come out of the furnace. Many hot glass bottles were put in each box. This made the boxes almost too heavy for children to carry.

Would you like to make a guess as to how long a child had to work in the factory each day? How many days a week do you think they worked? (Ask the listeners for their opinions.) The children worked twelve hours a day for six days a week! That would be like you going to school before sunrise every morning and working until sunset every evening, including Saturdays.

The only break the children got during the day was fifteen minutes for breakfast and 30 minutes for lunch. The day was too long, too dangerous and too hard. Do you think that these children had any time or energy left to go to school?

5 Working children did not always work in factories. Some children worked in fields picking vegetables, cotton or tobacco with their parents. Some children worked deep underground in coal mines. Children who worked were almost always tired, hungry, and often times sick from the bad conditions in which they worked. Plus, they did not have time to enjoy being kids. They had no time to climb trees, play tag, or fly kites.

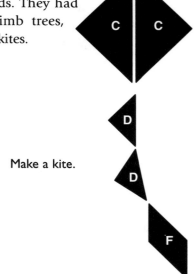

Make a kite.

They did not have time to go to school to learn skills so that they could get better jobs when they became adults.

6 Who helped these children? There were many people who were concerned about these children and the conditions in which they lived and worked. One of these people was Florence Kelley.

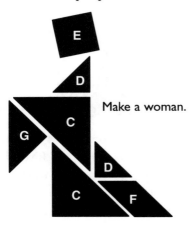

Make a woman.

All her life, Florence had been concerned about the working conditions of children.

In 1891, Florence Kelley was a divorced mother with three children. She moved to the busy city of Chicago where there were many factories. Florence saw children as young as five years old working in dark, dangerous factories and decided to try and change it. She thought that there should be laws against children working. But how would the people who made the laws know about the factories and the poor children who worked there?

Florence Kelley decided to write a report about this problem. In order to get the facts, she visited all types of factories. She also visited the neighborhoods where the factory workers lived. She talked to everyone she could about the problem. She asked children if they went to school or work. She asked parents how much money they made and if it was enough to buy food, clothes, and shelter for their families.

Florence spent all her time gathering information about these people, the factories they worked in, and the houses they lived in. Then she assembled the information into a long report. She included lots of facts and figures. But she also wrote true stories about the people she had met during her studies of the poor.

Florence Kelley gave her report to government officials and lawmakers. She wanted them to realize how important it was to make laws protecting children from harsh working conditions. She gave speeches at churches, clubs, and meetings. She encouraged people to go to the poor parts of the city and see for themselves what life was like for a child who had to work in a factory all day. She wanted everyone to know so that the lives of these poor people could be improved and made safer and easier.

Finally, in 1893, the lawmakers in Illinois passed laws that said that children could not work in factories if they were under the age of fourteen. The new laws also said that young people could not work more than eight hours a day. But would the factory owners follow the new laws? The lawmakers decided that someone needed to go from factory to factory and see if everyone was obeying the laws. Because of her knowledge and desire to help, Florence Kelley was appointed by the governor to be the very first Chief Factory Inspector.

Florence tried to get lawyers to help her make the factory bosses obey the child labor laws. But, most lawyers did not want to help. Florence decided that the best way she could help children was to become a lawyer herself. So she went to college and earned a degree in law. In the 1890s, it was very unusual for a woman to go to law school. But Florence did not let that stop her. In 1894, she graduated from law school.

7 Again, Florence Kelley spent the next four years visiting many different types of factories to make sure that the child labor laws were being followed.

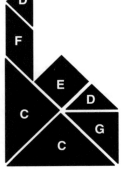

Make glass factory.

As you can imagine, many times she was unwelcome. Many factory owners hated her. Sometimes, her life was threatened. But she did not let that stop her.

In 1899, Florence returned to New York to become the head of the National Consumers' League. This organization was dedicated to letting people know how factory owners treated their workers. If the workers were treated badly, then people all across the United States were encouraged not to buy the things that the factory made. This would help force the factory owners to improve conditions for their workers.

Florence Kelley traveled all over the United States giving speeches and lectures so that people would know how hard life was for poor people and especially for children who worked in factories. Florence also started the United States Children's Bureau. Even today, this organization helps children, young babies and their mothers get needed food and medicines. The bureau also helps find homes for children who have no family to take care of them.

8 Florence Kelley dedicated her life to helping children who were forced to work because their families were poor.

She collected the facts and tried to make sure that people knew them. She urged the people to vote for laws to protect young children from working in factories or in other dangerous jobs.

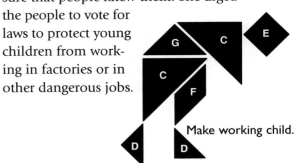

Make working child.

Today, Florence Kelley's work is still unfinished. In many parts of the world, young children must work long hours in bad conditions. There are also many people working to change this.

Florence Kelley was only one person, but through her dedication and hard work, she made a difference in the lives of thousands of children.

Activities & Discussion Questions

1. Florence Kelley helped children who worked in many different types of jobs. Choose three of the jobs that are mentioned in this story to make a flip booklet. Fold a piece of paper lengthwise. Divide paper into thirds. On one side, cut on the fold lines to the center of the paper. Now you have three doors that open to the other half of the paper. On the outside of each door, draw a child and a tool that he would use in his job. On the inside of this door, draw the factory or place that the child works in and write a short job description for him. Show it to your friends and see if they can guess what job is behind each door.

2. Today there are many laws protecting children. Some of the reasons for these laws are explained in the story. Find out if there are laws that affect when you can begin working. Look for the age when children are allowed to begin working in your community. Are there limits on where you can work? Or on how long you can work each week? Or on how late you can work? Suggestions on places to check include local businesses that employ students, the school and/or public library, and the Internet. Keep track of the time required to find the answer, and record what you learn so you can share your results.

3. Although there are many laws in the U.S. to protect children, this is not true in many poor countries where young children are still forced to work in factories? How could you locate more information on this? What could be done to protect these children.

4. Most children have chores to do around the house. Make a list of all the jobs that you do to help out and then ask your friends what jobs they do at their house. Take a poll of how many classmates take out the trash? How many friends are in charge of feeding their pet? How many are supposed to keep their room clean? Report your results to the class.

Super Search Question

The child labor laws researched in question 2 vary depending on where you live and how old the worker is. For example, by law a fourteen year old may not work as late or work as many hours as a seventeen year old. Do the additional research needed to collect information about ages and hours students can work. Make a bar graph to illustrate your results.

To learn more about Florence Kelley
Websites

► Florence Kelley: A Woman of Fierce Fidelity
http://www.idbsu.edu/socwork/dhuff/history/extras/Kelly.htm
A good overview of Florence Kelley's life and contributions to children's and women's rights, with illustrations.

► Florence Kelley
http://www.biography.com/cgi-bin/biomain.cgi
Provides a brief biography highlighting the key achievements of Florence Kelley's career as a social reformer.

Books/Nonfiction

Brill, Marlene. *Extraordinary Young People.* Children's Press, 1996. Biographical accounts of noteworthy individuals who accomplished remarkable achievements at an early age.

Currie, Stephen. *We Have Marched Together: The Working Children's Crusade.* Lerner, 1997. Focuses on protest march from Philadelphia to New York City, with photographs of children at work.

Freedman, Russell. *Kids at Work: Lewis Hine and the Crusade Against Child Labor.* Clarion, 1998. Photobiography of early twentieth century photographer Lewis Hine.

Saller, Carol. *Florence Kelley.* Carolrhoda, 1997. Written for children ages 4–8, this biography of Florence Kelley also includes historical information about child labor in the United States.

Books/Fiction

Cochrane, Patricia. *Purely Rosie Pearl.* Delacorte, 1996. A twelve-year-old girl gives an account of her daily life as part of a migrant family.

Paterson, Katerine. *Lyddie.* Lodestar, 1991. The story of a young Vermont farm girl who goes to work in the factories of Lowell, Massachusetts.

Ross, Pat. *Hannah's Fancy Notions.* Viking Kestrel, 1992. Hannah sets out to make something special for her sister, who works to support the family.

Juliette Gordon Low

Girls, raise your hand if you have ever been a Girl Scout, or a Brownie? Perhaps when you were in kindergarten you were a Daisy. This is how you say **Daisy** in sign language. Daisies are the very youngest group of Girl Scouts. This is how you say **yes** in sign language. Say **yes** in sign language if you were a Daisy.

Even if you are a boy, your life has been touched by Girl Scouts. Perhaps your mother was a Girl Scout, or your sister, or cousin. I bet you have eaten lots of Girl Scout cookies in your life. Say **Yes** in sign language if you have.

Girl Scouts, Brownies and **Daisies** were started by Juliette Gordon Low in 1912. At that time she was 52 years old and completely deaf. But she did not let anything stop her efforts to help girls all over the United States.

Let's talk for a minute about what **Daisies**, Brownies, and Girl Scouts do, besides sell those wonderful cookies every year. Who can tell me something that Girl Scouts do? *(Discuss answers, such as visits to the elderly, make gifts for underprivileged children, plant trees in parks.)*

Girl Scouts is a world wide organization that encourages girls to develop their interests and abilities and to be good citizens. This is sign language for **girl** and **scout**. Can you do these signs with me? The **Girl Scouts** participate in educational work and play activities of all types including boating, hiking, nature study, games, handicrafts, hobbies, and camping. In some countries, Girl Scouts are called Girl Guides.

Juliette Gordon Low was a very interesting person. Born in Savannah, Georgia, in 1860, she grew up right in the middle of the Civil War. She had three sisters and two brothers. Her parents named her Juliette. But when her uncle saw her for the first time, he thought that she was so cute that he called her a **daisy**. So, from then on, everyone called her **Daisy**.

As Daisy grew up, she became very daring and would try anything. Her sister called her "**Crazy Daisy**." This is the sign language for **crazy**. When she was eight, **Daisy** pulled a little boy from a pool of water, saving his life. She took care of any stray dogs and cats, injured birds or any other animal that came her way.

As a teenager, she left home to attend school. She went first to Virginia and then to New York City. After graduation, she went on a trip to Europe. There she met some friends of her family and their son, William Low. He was about her age and they fell in love. Two years later, he came to America to meet her family. They were married in a grand ceremony, complete with a beautiful dress for Juliette and many bridesmaids to throw rice on the happy couple for good luck.

But, as William and Juliette ran through a storm of rice, one grain of rice accidentally got stuck in her ear. This is how you do the sign for **ear**. Her **ear** became infected because of that grain of rice. Today, if you have an **ear** infection, there are many different medicines to help you get well. But, unfortunately for Juliette, her **ear** infection led to deafness in that ear. What made things worse for her was that she had already developed a severe hearing loss in her other **ear** just the year before.

Juliette Low would now be deaf for the rest of her life. But she did not let that stop her from having fun. After Juliette and her new husband moved back to Europe, they lived in his family homes in both England and Scotland. She entertained her new European friends with her Southern cooking and parties. She kept busy, enjoying lots of parties and traveling back and forth from England to the United States to see her family.

Juliette went home to her family when the Spanish-American War broke out. Her father was a general in the war and her brothers were aides to their father. Juliette and her mother helped care for the sick and wounded soldiers. They all did such a fine job that the President of the United States commended, or officially praised, the entire family.

After the war, Juliette painted and sculpted and wrote poetry. She even learned how to be a blacksmith—a person who makes things from metal. Then Daisy's husband died and she felt very alone. She did not have any children to care for and felt that she should do something useful with the rest of her life. But she did not know what to do.

During one of her trips to England, she met General Sir Robert Baden-Powell. He had left his post in the British army to begin the Boy Scouts in 1907. He wanted to give boys training in citizenship, learning new things and helping others. Baden-Powell's sister, Agnes, had started the Girl Guides because so many girls wanted to belong to a group like the Boy Scouts.

The more Juliette learned about the Girl Guides, the more she wanted to start her own group. So she organized a group of seven girls at her home in Scotland. Soon after that, she started two more girls groups in London, England. Juliette was happy because she had found a way to help others. This is the sign language for **help**. Can you do the sign for **help** with me?

Juliette returned home to America to start a Girl Guides, group in Savannah. General Baden-Powell was also going to the United States as part of the worldwide tour to promote the Boy Scouts. They traveled on the same ship together and he helped Juliette plan her own **Girl Scouts**. As soon as she got home, she started two groups in Savannah. Then she planned the uniforms, projects, and activities for the girls.

Juliette Low worked very hard on her **Girl Scouts**. She wanted Girl Scouts to be in every state in our nation. In order to do this, she needed a national organization, so she set up a headquarters in Washington, D.C. She wrote a handbook for Girl Scout leaders which gave them information about the organization, its goals, uniforms and activities.

Juliette asked her friends in important places to help. She even asked Mrs. Woodrow Wilson, Mrs. Hoover and Mrs. Coolidge, the wives of United States presidents for their help in getting Girl Scouts started. Everyone said "**Yes**" to Juliette's requests for help. Do you remember how to say the word "**yes**" in sign language?

Juliette never heard the word "**No**" from anyone she asked. This is how you say "**no**" in sign language. Remember that all this time, Juliette was completely deaf. But she never let her handicap stand in her way or prevent her from communicating with people.

For many years, Juliette traveled all over the United States helping girls and volunteer scout leaders start new troops. She spent much of her own money so that the new **Girl Scouts** could have handbooks and uniforms.

In 1926, a World Camp in London was started for **Girl Scouts** all over the world. Their goal was to work toward world peace.

Juliette Low died in 1927 in Savannah, Georgia. She had worked tirelessly for over sixteen years for girls all over the world. She herself had truly lived by the **Girl Scout** Promise. Perhaps you have heard this promise. It goes like this:

> *On my honor, I will try:*
> *To serve God and my country,*
> *To help people at all times,*
> *And to live by the Girl Scout Law.*

Do you remember the sign language for **help**? Can you do this with me? The sign for **people** is this. Do this sign with me. The sign for **always**, which we can use for the phrase 'at all times' is this. Make this sign with me. Now let's put these signs together and sign "**To help people at all times.**" That's exactly right. And that's what Juliette Low tried to do with her Girl Scouts.

Today, Girl Scouts celebrate Juliette Low's birthday which is on October 31. It is their way to say **thank you** to Juliette for starting Girl Scouts. This is how you say **thank you** in sign language. October 31 is called Founder's Day. It is in honor of the one woman who helped girls all over the world, despite her deafness.

Activities & Discussion Questions

1. Try adding a few more words to your sign language vocabulary. Using one of the sign language dictionaries (listed in the resources below) or an Internet source, such as the **Sign Language Dictionary Online** (http://dww.deafworldweb.org/asl/index.html) look up a common word such as please, thank you, cat or dog.

2. Girl Scouts is now a large international organization. Visit the Girl Scouts of the USA home page (http://www.girlscouts.org/) to find out more information about this organization. How many girls and adult volunteers are members the Girl Scouts of the USA *(Answer: 3.5 million, including 2.6 million girls)* and how many nations have chapters of the Girl Scouts *(Answer: 136)*.

3. Participation in Girl Scout or Brownies was an important part of many young girls childhood. Are you in Girl Scouts? Ask your mother, sister, aunt, or neighbor if they were ever a Girl Scout or Brownie. Ask them what activities they participated in with their troop.

4. Can you name any other organizations that were founded to guide girls and boys? Where could you locate more information about these organizations? *(Answers include: Girls Inc. (girlsinc.org; 4-H (fourhcouncil.edu); YMCA (ymca.net); YWCA (ywca.org); and Junior Achievement (ja.org).*

Super Search Question

Find the home pages for the other organizations for boys and girls that you named in question 4. List these.

To learn more about Juliette Low & Sign Language
Websites

► Girl Scouts of the USA Home Page
http:// www.girlscouts.org/

News and other information on the Girl Scouts in the United States.

► Juliette Gordon (Low)
http://www.girlscouts.org/girls/GS/jgl/jglself.htm
This page has a color photo of Juliette as a girl with a link to a picture of her childhood home.

► Juliette Gordon Low
http://www.zia.org/jglow.htm
A brief biography of Juliette Low and her contributions. From Zia Girl Scout Council.

► World Association of Girl Guides and Girl Scouts
http://wagggsworld.org/
History of the organization in several languages, and a description of current projects.

Books

Behrens, June. *Juliette Low.* Children's Press, 1885.

Brown, Fern. *Daisy and the Girl Scouts.* Whitman and Albert, 1996.

Lawrence, Daisy. *The Lady from Savannah.* Girl Scout Press, 1988.

Pace, Mildred Mastin. *Juliette Low.* Jesse Stuart Foundation, 1997.

Smith, Shari Steel. *Juliette Gordon Low.* Parenting Press, 1990.

Sign Language Resources

Costello, Elaine, and Lois Lenderman. *Random House American Sign Language Dictionary.* Random House, 1994.

Sternberg, Martin. *American Sign Language: A Comprehensive Dictionary.* HarperCollins, 1981.

Daisy

Mime plucking flower petals with RH "G" from LH "1".

Yes

"S"-Shape RH. Shake up and down at wrist.

Crazy

Circle RH index finger 3x at temple.

Ear

Pinch right ear lobe with RH index and thumb. Other fingers closed.

Girl

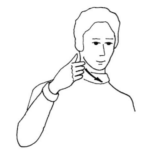

Move RH "A" shape down jaw line.

Scout

Hold up RH index, middle and fourth fingers.

No

Quickly snap RH index, middle finger and thumb together

Help

Place LH "A," thumb up, in RH palm. Raise both hands.

People

Alternate both hands "P" shapes in a circular motion.

Always

Circle 3x RH "1" shape.

Thank You

Place RH fingertips on lips. Then move outward as if throwing a kiss.

Maria Montessori

Did you go to preschool when you were little? If you did not go to preschool, I bet you went to kindergarten. Do you remember some of the fun things that you did there? Can you tell us your favorite activity? Some of the learning games that you worked with in kindergarten or preschool were not just the regular toys that you can buy today at a department store. They were special learning games, puzzles or toys that were made just for children to use in school. You learned a lot by working with them, didn't you? And you had fun.

But 100 years ago, kindergarten was not fun. Children wore very stiff and tight uniforms. They sat on hard benches. The girls were in one classroom and the boys were in another separate classroom.

Their classroom did not look at all like your classroom does today. There were no pictures on the walls. The children had very few books to read and these books had no pictures. The children did not have any writing materials; no paper, no chalk, no pencils. All day long they sat up straight and looked at the teacher. No child was ever allowed to talk. No student was allowed to ask questions. The teachers read the lesson to the students and then the students had to repeat exactly what they said. If a student accidentally made a mistake, the lesson had to be repeated over and over again, until it was exactly perfect.

Children were not allowed to think for themselves. Their schools had no toys or learning games of any kind. Do you think that you would like to go to this type of school? Do you think that learning would be fun?

Schools have made wonderful changes since then. How did these improvements come about? There is one woman whose ideas and teaching methods changed schools forever. Her name was Maria Montessori. Perhaps you have heard of Montessori schools or even attended one yourself when you were younger.

Maria spent most of her life doing something that she thought she would never do, and that is teach. She thought that teachers were very boring people. You can understand her feelings if you remember the type of schools that she attended.

Maria achieved wonderful things in her life, but not all at once. She just took small steps along the way.

When she was twelve years old in Rome, Italy, she took her first step. **(1. Fold paper and cut first step.)** Maria decided to go to a boys' high school because she wanted to learn math. Girls went to separate schools and were not taught math. Of course, her family was shocked and did not approve. Girls were not supposed to like math! But Maria convinced her parents to let her go.

Four years later, Maria graduated from the boys' high school and took her next step. **(2. Cut next step.)** She went to the University of Rome for two years. She became an engineer.

Her family was surprised again when Maria announced that she had changed her mind about being an engineer. Now she wanted to be a doctor! There were no women doctors in Italy. But Maria did not let that stop her. It wasn't easy but she enrolled in medical school. After four long years of study, Maria became a medical doctor. At age 26, she was the first woman doctor in Italy. This was really a big step, not only for Maria but also for other women who were interested in becoming doctors. **(3. Cut third step.)**

Then Maria was invited to speak at an international women's conference. She was a wonderful speaker and her audience loved her. She spoke out for the right of women to make their own career choices and to look beyond marriage for a more fulfilling life. This was the beginning of Maria's lifelong commitment to improving the rights of women. For example, Maria thought that women should have the same pay as men, if they do the same jobs as men.

As a doctor, Maria enjoyed treating children the most. She also became the director of a school for mentally handicapped children in Rome. It was in this position that she took her next big step. **(4. Cut fourth step.)**

She developed new teaching tools to use with these children. The new games that she developed encouraged children to learn by using their hands, their eyes, their ears and their minds. The children were allowed to ask questions, work on projects as long as they liked, and talk to the other children in their class. The mentally handicapped children in Maria Montessori's school learned so much that they passed the reading and writing test which was given to normal children.

Maria wanted to try her new teaching and learning methods with children in regular schools. Maria got her chance when she was asked to teach 50 of the poorest children of the city. She called her new school "Children's House." All day long the children sorted objects and counted them. They stacked up blocks in order. They put triangle shapes into triangle spaces, and squares into square spaces. They sat in child-sized chairs and worked at child-size tables. They had books to look at and chalkboards for drawing. The children were free to find out things for themselves. Montessori's new teaching methods were incredibly successful.

Less than two years later, Maria opened more schools using her teaching methods and materials. She wrote a book and gave lectures on her new ways to teach children. Many visitors came to visit her schools to learn more.

Soon Montessori schools were springing up, not only in Italy, but also in the rest of the world. Maria spent the rest of her life traveling throughout the world, giving lectures about children and how to teach them.

Maria's last big step was when she was nominated for the Nobel Peace Prize for her lifelong commitment to the education of children. She was nominated three times, in 1949, 1950, and 1951 for this honor. **(5. Cut last step.)**

Maria Montessori did not set out to climb as high as a mountain, or to accomplish so many important things. She just took one step at a time. **(Open out steps.)** These steps also look much like the building blocks that the children in Montessori schools use to learn about the concept of small, medium and large. Have you ever put blocks in a stack like this?

When Maria died at the age of 81, she was famous all over the world as the woman who improved schools for children. She herself taught the world what childhood is about, and how important a time childhood is in everyone's life. She also helped the world understand how children learn.

Today there are many official Montessori schools all over the world. Almost all these schools use Maria Montessori's ideas that children should have a pleasant, safe, and happy place in which to learn and grow.

Maria Montessori was just one woman, yet her ideas have helped your school be a better place for you.

Activities & Discussion Questions

1. Many of the toys and games that children play with today were not available to the children whom Montessori taught. With a partner, make a list of all of these toys. Then make a second list of things that children of both then and now like to play with.

2. Think back to when you went to kindergarten or preschool. What was your favorite thing to do or play with? Write a short paragraph describing your favorite toy, game or activity. If you could go back to kindergarten for one day, what activity, game, toy or book would you most like to get involved with?

3. Glue or paste the letters in Montessori's name (already cut out) onto a poster board. Then, under-neath each letter, write the name of a game or toy that begins with that letter. For example, you could write mop for M because children like to play with child-size mops. Ring toss is a toy that starts with R.

4. If you stood at the door of your school's kindergarten and just watched what is going on, you would see children playing, singing songs, or listening to stories. Are they learning things while doing these activities? Write down some questions about kindergarten that you could ask the teacher. These might include what each child needs to learn in kindergarten in order to be successful in first grade, how the teacher helps children learn, and what his or her favorite subject to teach is.

Check with your teacher to see if you can arrange an interview with the kindergarten teacher.

Super Search Question

Maria Montessori was nominated three different times (1949, 1950, and 1951) for a Nobel Prize for her commitment to the education of children. Use the library's reference books and the Internet to get information on the Nobel Prizes, and see if Maria Montessori ever received the award for her contributions to education. *(Answer: The easiest resource to use is the World Almanac, which lists all the Nobel Prize winners. There is no award category for education, and that may be one of the reasons why Maria Montessori never won the Nobel Prize.)*

To learn more about Maria Montessori
Websites

► Montessori Online
http://www.montessori.org
The Home Page of the Montessori Foundation, containing a directory of schools, resources, calendar, and other links.

► Maria Montessori and Informal Education
http://www.infed.org/thinkers/et-mont.htm
A brief biography on Maria Montessori with links to other Internet resources.

► Maria Montessori: An Appreciation
http://transporter.com/mcc/essay01.htm
A biographical assessment posted on the Montessori Catholic Council Home Page.

► Teacher Hero: Maria Montessori
http://www.myhero.com/hero.asp?hero=MariaMontessori
From the Brickton Montessori School. Sixth Year Class.

Books

Knauer, Kelly, ed. *Great People of the Twentieth Century.* Time, 1996.

Kramer, Rita. *Maria Montessori: A Biography.* University of Chicago Press, 1976.

Shephard, Marie Tennent. *Maria Montessori: Teacher of Teachers.* Lerner, 1996. Biography with many period photographs of Montessori, her associates, and students.

Maria Montessori

Note:
Use a primary color such as
red, blue, or green.

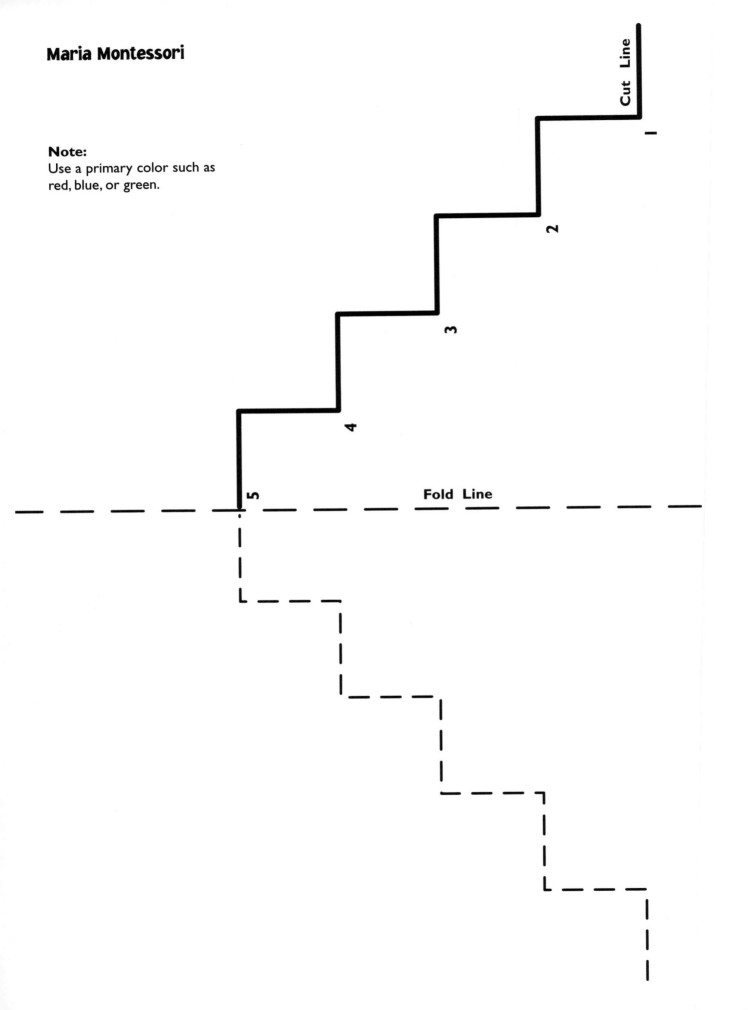

Mother Teresa

We are going to use sign language to tell this story about Mother Teresa, a very small woman with a very big heart. This is the sign for **small** and this is the sign for **big**. You can see how the signs are related. Let's do these signs together.

Mother Teresa was a **nun**. Here is the sign for **Mother**. We can use the sign for the letter "T" to represent the name **Teresa**. Here is the sign for **nun**. Will you do these signs with me. Great! **Mother Teresa** set out alone to improve life for people. Do you know how she did it? She did it by helping just **one person** at a time—the person nearest to her. The sign language for **one person** is this. **Mother Teresa** helped just **one person** at a time. This is the sign for **help**.

Here's the story:

Mother Teresa started life on August 26, 1910, as Agnes Gonxha Bojaxhu (pronounced *Gon-ja Boya-joo*) in what is now Yugoslavia. She had an older brother named Lazar (pronounced *La-zar*) and an older sister, whose name was Age (pronounced *A-gee*). Her father was a good provider for his family and her mother raised her children kindly, strictly and religiously.

When Agnes was ten, her father died suddenly. Without her father's income, the family became poor. To earn money, her mother sold hand embroidery and cloth. But Agnes' mother still had time to **help** lonely or sick neighbors. She often said to Agnes, "Do good as if you were tossing a pebble into the sea."

When Agnes was 18, she wanted to become a missionary in India, so she decided to become a **nun**. She traveled to Ireland to learn English. Then she went to Calcutta, India, to teach the children of British tea plantation owners.

Agnes chose the name of **Teresa** after another **nun** who had lived many years ago in France.

The earlier Sister Teresa had written that it is possible to serve God by doing ordinary, simple jobs with cheerfulness and joy. She adopted this wonderful philosophy. As Agnes, now **Sister Teresa**, put her heart into everything she did. She often said, "Do small things with great love."

We can say this famous quote in sign language. This is the sign for **do**. Let's make this sign together. The sign for **small** is this. Can you make this sign with me? This is the sign for **things**. Let's do this sign together. This is the sign for *with*. Good job making this sign. **Great** is made like this. You might already know the sign for **love**. Do these signs with me.

Now let's put all these signs together and sign Mother Teresa's famous saying. "**Do all things with great love**". Good job. We can keep this idea of hers in mind as we learn about what she accomplished in her life as a **nun**.

In 1937, **Sister Teresa** took her final vows to become a nun. She continued her teaching at the convent. Later, she became principal of the convent school.

In 1948, **Sister Teresa** felt called by God to **help** the poor outside her convent walls. She had to wait a year to get permission to leave the convent because a **nun** was not allowed to go outside the convent walls. Finally, she was granted permission.

After spending twenty years behind the walls of the safe convent, **Sister Teresa** said a tearful goodbye and walked out of the convent that she had loved for so long. She was 38 years old. She had no money. She had no place to live. But she did have faith. She had faith that God would take care of her. Armed only with her faith, she walked into the dirty, smelly streets of Calcutta, India. Let's make the sign for **sister** together.

At first, **Sister Teresa** was overwhelmed by the sight of so many people—many of whom were in great need. She felt frustrated because she could not **help** everyone. Then she remembered the philosophy of the French **nun**. **Sister Teresa** reminded herself that she needed only to **"Do small things with great love."** Do you remember these signs?

Whom should she **help** first? She started with the smallest **person** she saw—a child.

Sister Teresa smoothed out a patch of dirt and wrote some letters of the alphabet in the dirt with a stick. She talked to the child about the letters.

Soon a second child and then a third, fourth, and a fifth child came over to see what they were doing. **Sister Teresa's** school grew as more and more children came to her each day.

Sister Teresa not only taught the children about the letters of the alphabet, she taught them to **love** one another. She taught them how to wash and showed them what soap was. Many children had never even seen a bar of soap! In all of this, **Sister Teresa** was **doing small things with great love**.

When people found out about the school, they **helped** out by giving her things like tables, old books, and a few chairs. Soon, former convent students came to join **Sister Teresa** in her work with the poor and sick. So many **nuns** came to **help** her that church officials in Rome decided that **Sister Teresa** could establish a new order of **nuns**. It was called Missionaries of Charity and **Sister Teresa** was now to be called **Mother Teresa**.

The home where the **Sisters** lived was becoming crowded, so they moved to a new location. She also opened a home for orphaned and abandoned children, a home for teenage mothers, clinics for victims of leprosy, and a food program for the poor. **Mother Teresa** continued to **do small things with great love**.

In 1960, **Mother Teresa** began traveling outside India to let the whole world know that the poor needed help. She criss-crossed the world, raising money for the poor and setting up centers for the Missionaries of Charity. She traveled to the United States and discussed plans to build homes for AIDS victims and the homeless.

Then, in 1979, **Mother Teresa** won the Nobel Peace Prize, one of the greatest prizes in the world. She traveled to Norway to receive the prize. She accepted the honor and the publicity, not for herself, but for the world's poorest and sickest people. She was given $190,000 which she used to buy food and shelter for these people. She requested that the $6,000 that was normally spent on the award banquet be given to the poor instead. That money bought food for 15,000 hungry people. People marveled at how such a **small person** could accomplish such **big things**!

President Reagan gave the Presidential Medal of Freedom to **Mother Teresa** in 1985. She was also made an honorary United States citizen. Despite all the attention given to her and all the many medals she won, **Mother Teresa** never changed her goal—Do small things with great love.

The many **small things** added together amounted to a great life achievement. Through her example, Mother Teresa showed how **one person** truly can **help** the entire world. Today, there are Missionaries of Charity in 87 countries. Best of all, the story of **Mother Teresa** inspires all of us to contribute in our own small way.

When someone once asked her what they could do to **help**, Mother Teresa said, "Begin at home by saying something good to your child, to your husband, or to your wife. Begin by **helping** someone in need in your community, at work, or at school. Begin by making whatever you do become something beautiful for others."

Mother Teresa died on September 5, 1997, at the age of 87. All her life she had said, "We can do no great things—only **small things with great love**." **Mother Teresa** spent her life showing that **one person** can make a difference.

Activities & Discussion Questions

1. President Reagan gave Mother Teresa the Presidential Medal of Freedom. Using the resources in your library, learn more about this award.

2. There is information about Mother Teresa on the My Hero website (http://www.myhero.com). There are links to other Nobel Peace Prize winners. Using this source, learn more Mother Teresa and the other winners.

3. Even though there were many people whom Mother Teresa wanted to help, she started out by helping just one child learn the letters of the alphabet. Each one of us can make a big difference by helping out and being kind to the people around us. Go to the **Random Acts of Kindness** website (http://www.acts ofkindness.org) and learn more about this organization devoted to encouraging people to be kind to one another. There are lots of ideas about how you can get your school involved in Random Acts of Kindness Week.

4. Mother Teresa dedicated her life to helping the poorest people in India. How might her ideas be used today to continue her work? Are there other places with the same kinds of problems Mother Teresa saw in India? Where would you begin?

Super Search Question

What year did Mother Teresa receive the Nobel Peace Prize? She also received many other awards in recognition of her work. Using resources in the school media center, find the year she received the Nobel Prize and find at least one other award she was given. *(Answer: Nobel, 1979. Presidential Medal of Freedom and Congressional Gold Medal, Albert Schweitzer Humanitarian Award.)*

To learn more about Mother Teresa
Websites

► Mother Teresa
http://www.tisv.be/mt/indmt.htm
Comprehensive website with links to biographical information on Mother Teresa, books, awards, prayers and more.

► Mother Teresa of India
http://www.netsrq.com/~dbois/m-teresa.html
Brief biographical article on Mother Teresa. From Microsoft Encarta.

Books

Giff, Patricia Reilly. *Mother Teresa: Sister to the Poor.* (Women of Our time). Viking Press, 1986.

Johnson, Linda Carson. *Mother Teresa: Protector of the Sick.* Blackbirch Press, 1991.

Pond, Mildred M. *Mother Teresa.* Chelsea Juniors, 1992. Biography with quotations.

The Poor. Raintree/SteckVaughn, 1998. Biography with dateline, bibliography and glossary.

Wheeler, Jill. *Mother Teresa.* Abdo & Daughters, 1992.

Articles

Bryson, Donna. "Mother Teresa's Sainthood Mulled." *U.S. News and World Report.* Sept 9, 1997.

Noonan, Peggy. "Woman of the World" *Reader's Digest.* December, 1997: 122-124.

Satchell, Michael. "Death Comes to a Living Saint." *U.S. News and World Report.* Sept. 15, 1997: 12.

CD-ROM

"Mother Teresa of India." *Microsoft Encarta.* Microsoft, 1998. CD-ROM.

Mother

RH "5" shape. Place thumb on chin and wiggle fingers.

"T"

Nun

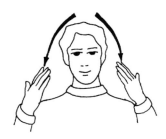

Move open-faced hands down along both sides of head as if outlining nun's habit.

One

Person

"P"-shape both hands. Slide wrists down against sides of body.

Help

Place LH "A," thumb up, in RH palm. Raise both hands.

Sister

LH palm down, "1" shape, tip out. Place RH thumb on right cheek, then change to "1" shape and place next to LH.

Do

Swing claw-shaped hands back and forth.

Small

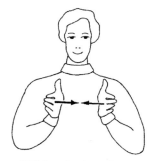

Open "B" hands, then draw together.

Things

Open "B" RH palm up. In small bouncing movements, move out and to the right.

With

"A"-shape hands, then bring together.

Great (big)

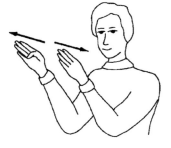

"B"-shape hands, palms facing, then move hands apart.

Love

Cross "S"-shape hands, and place over heart.

John Muir

John Muir once said, "The mountains are calling me and I must go."

Ever since he could remember, John was trying to escape into nature. John Muir was born in 1838 in Scotland, but he moved to America in 1849 when he was eleven years old. His family settled on a farm in Wisconsin. Farming was very hard work and John's father was unusually strict. After his chores were done, John enjoyed slipping into the woods or wading in a nearby stream. John taught himself to swim by watching frogs swim, observed animals taking care of their young, and studied all the different plants and animals around him. He loved and respected all the creatures on his family's farm.

This is the sign for **nature**. Can you do it with me? It seemed to John that he could hear **nature** calling to him. Perhaps it sounded something like this:

The **woods** called to John,
The **animals** called to John,
"We want you to **come** out and **play**.
Enjoy our fragile **beauty**.
Preserve us for a future day.
We think this is your **duty**.

We can express some of these words in sign language. This is the sign for **woods**. Can you do this with me? This the sign for **animals**. Can you do this sign with me? This is the sign for **come** and this is the sign **play**. Do these signs with me. These are the signs for **beauty, preserve, day**. Let's do these signs together. As we learn about John Muir and his life, we can say this poem and do these signs.

When John was not outside enjoying nature, he was inside inventing things to make his chores easier so that he could spend more time outside. He invented a sawmill, barometer and a trick bed. The bed was designed to dump the sleeping person out on the floor at a pre-set hour.

When he was 22 years old, he took his inventions to the state fair in Madison, Wisconsin and won a cash prize for them. He decided to stay in Madison and study geology and botany at the University of Wisconsin. To pay for college, he earned money doing odd jobs.

Soon the Civil War started and John's classmates talked about it constantly. John was against fighting and decided to go to medical school and become a doctor so that he could help the sick and wounded soldiers. In order to escape all the talk of war, he took long walks in the woods and collected all types of plants to draw and study.

John was afraid that he would be drafted into the army if he stayed in the United States. To avoid fighting, he headed north to Canada and the "University of the Wilderness" as he called it. **(Say the poem together.)**

After the Civil War ended, John moved to Indianapolis, to work and be near the vast Indiana forests. He worked for a company that manufactured carriage parts. He used his skills to invent machines that increased production and saved the company money. He also made suggestions on how to increase worker efficiency.

John was on his way to a successful career in industry when he suffered a serious injury to his eye. A sharp file flew out of his hand while he was tightening a machine belt. During his recovery, John had lots of time to think about his future. Did he want to spend his life in a factory looking at machines, or outside looking at all the beautiful plants and animals? John could make lots of money as an industrialist or very little money as a naturalist. John could heard nature calling to him. **(Let's say our poem again.)**

He gave up his job in Indianapolis and went on a three year journey into nature. He walked to Florida. Then he moved to California. While he was in California, he herded sheep to make money and explored the Yosemite Valley. It was easy for John to see how plants, animals, soil and water were all interconnected. He said that nature is "one living, pulsing organism."

John Muir became known as an expert on Yosemite and studied the living glaciers there. In 1864, California accepted a grant from President Lincoln that set aside 62 square miles at Yosemite, creating the first wilderness area in the United States.

As more and more people moved into the Yosemite area, trees hundreds of years old were cut down and meadows were damaged by too many grazing sheep and cows. John spent many hours writing articles and stories about his experiences in the wilderness. He became well-known throughout the United States. He gave lectures about the importance of preserving nature and about the importance of expanding Yosemite into a national park. He wanted other people to also be in tune with nature and recognized that everyone needed some time to enjoy our outdoor wonders. **(Say poem.)**

In 1890, Congress designated a total of 1,200 square miles of Yosemite as a National Park. Congress also created Sequoia and Grant National Parks in order to preserve large stands of giant sequoia trees. John was pleased that his recommendations to preserve nature were answered.

During this busy time, John got married and ran the fruit farm that his in-laws owned. He also had two daughters. His work and family responsibilities kept him from spending as much time as he wanted in the wilderness. But whenever John felt that he needed a break, he would go out into nature for relaxation and enjoyment.

Some of John's own family members moved to California to help him with the fruit farm. This gave John more time to start a hiking and nature club. John was elected president of the Sierra Club which became one of the most powerful conservation organizations in the world. John became a leader of many land preservation battles.

In 1903, President Teddy Roosevelt came out to California to visit and camp with John Muir. John helped President Roosevelt understand the importance of preserving as much wilderness as possible. After this trip, Roosevelt tripled the land area of the national forests and doubled the number of national parks in our country. **(Say poem.)**

When Muir took his daughter Helen to Arizona so that she could recover from pneumonia, he again studied nature. He discovered a forest of petrified wood, which is wood that had been turned into stone over thousands of years. John brought this wonderful stone forest to national attention, and President Roosevelt created the Petrified Forest National Monument and the Grand Canyon National Monument.

When Muir died in 1914, he had been working on a book about his travels in Alaska. This book and many of his other journals, essays, and letters were published and are still read today.

John Muir became known as the "father of our national parks." Today, millions of Americans enjoy the wondrous and varied beauties of nature in our national parks. John Muir was one man, yet he contributed to millions of people's enjoyment of nature. **(Let's say our poem one last time.)**

Activities & Discussion Questions

1. Have you ever been to a national park? Using the National Park Service website (http://www.nps.gov/parks.html) find out how many national park units there are in your state. Look under "Find a Park by State Map." Click on your state and learn about the national parks near you. Each park has its own page with information about why the park is a special place worth preserving and the things that you can do there.

2. The story mentions the Sierra Club, which was founded by John Muir. Today this is a major organization devoted to environmental protection. However, not everyone believes that the work they do is best for our country. Check for more information so that you can have a class discussion. Check in the school media center for books and articles on the Sierra Club activities. One of the best places for current information is the Sierra Club's website (http://www.sierraclub. org/).

3. One of the most recent controversies involving the national parks has been efforts by conservationists to reintroduce a number of previously threatened wildlife species back into the parks. For example, wolves have been released in several parks. Farmers and cattle ranchers are opposed to this because they fear the wolves will attach the cattle and other livestock near the parks. How do you feel about this controversy?

4. During the course of his life, John Muir traveled all over the United States. John Muir started his life in Wisconsin as a child after leaving Scotland with his family. When he became an adult, he moved to Canada, then Indiana, then Florida, and finally California. Use the information in the story and a map of the United States to trace John's travels throughout his life.

Super Search Question

President Teddy Roosevelt was mentioned in the story as an early advocate of conservation, and for expanding the national park system. What was the first national park and when was it created? *(Answer: Congress established Yellowstone National Park in 1872.)*

To learn more about John Muir
Websites

► John Muir
http://www.Sierraclub.org/history/muir
Facts on John Muir and the Sierra Club, as well as an exhibit and study guide. From the Sierra Club.

► John Muir National Historic Site
http://www.nps.gov/jomu/
This page has information from the National Park Service about the Muir's home in California.

► John Muir Centre
http://www.cs.strath.ac.uk/contrib/JMC
News on conservation related events, awards and issues.

► Earthkeeper Hero: John Muir
http://www.myhero.com
Biography with links to Yosemite. Grades 2–5. From Harold W. Wood, Jr.

► John Muir:-Earth Planet Universe.
http://www.terraquest.com/highsights/valley/muir.html
Brief biographical information with photographs.

Books

Anderson, Peter. *John Muir: Wilderness Prophet.* (First Books: American Conservationists Series) Franklin Watts, 1996.

Dunham, Montrew. *John Muir: Young Naturalist.* (Childhood of Famous Americans) Aladdin, 1996.

Greene, Carol. *John Muir: Man of the Wild Places.* (Rookie Biography). Children's Press, 1991. Gr. 1–3.

Nadine, Corinne. *John Muir: Saving the Wilderness.* (Gateway Biography) Millbrook Press, 1994. Simple to read text, easy language.

Articles

Fleming, Candace. "Bully for Yosemite!" *Highlights for Children.* 15 August, 1996.

Nature (environment)

Circle RH "E" shape counterclock-wise around LH index finger.

Woods (tree)

Place back of LH under R elbow. Rapidly twist and shake RH "5" shape.

Animals

Move claw hands back and forth on upper chest.

Come

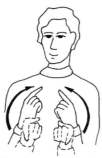

Knuckles down, index fingers out. Bring hands up and point to chest.

Play

Twist "Y" shaped hands back and forth, palms in.

Beauty

Circle face with RH palm in "5" shape. End in "O" shape. Then open fingers while moving hand away from chin.

Preserve (save)

Tap back of LH "V" with tips of RH "V."

Day

Place elbow of RH "D" on open LH, and arc RH "D" down to left elbow.

Think

Make tiny circle with index finger at forehead.

Duty (work)

Palms down, "S" shape hands. Hit back of LH with RH 2x.

Louis Pasteur

1 Over 100 years ago, Louis Pasteur started a fight against disease, and scientists all over the world continue this battle today. They continue his research in an area of study that is now called microbiology. It all started with a curious little boy in a small town in France.

In 1830, Louis was eight years and was fishing with a friend one hot summer day. Suddenly, they heard screams. A little neighbor girl was crying, "A wolf bit me. Help! Help!"

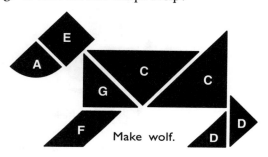

Make wolf.

Louis and his friend helped Annette home and then ran to get the doctor. As he ran, Louis remembered that eight people in his village had already died after being bitten by this wolf. The wolf had rabies, a sickness that makes animals go crazy and bite other animals and people.

Louis asked everyone, "Why does one animal get rabies and not another one? What causes it? Why do people get it after being bitten by a rabid animal?" But no one knew the answers to these questions. And no one knew how to find out either.

2 Louis continued to ask all kinds of questions, both out of school and in school.

Make schoolhouse.

He worked slowly and carefully in school at all his assignments. Louis particularly liked science and art. He drew portraits of his family, and friends. The pictures that he drew were particularly wonderful because Louis captured the spirit of the person by observing very closely all the important details about that person.

3 When he was twenty, Louis went to college in order to become a science teacher. He also continued with his drawing lessons.

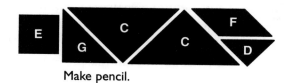

Make pencil.

In 1849, when Louis was 26, he became a chemistry professor and got married. The year before, he had made some important discoveries about crystals by using his powers of careful observation. Now his new wife, Marie, helped him with his work. They made a good team. They also had a wonderful family life with five children. Louis continued to study crystals until some of his fellow Frenchmen asked for his help.

Many people in France made their living by making alcohol from beet juice. The alcohol was used to make perfume, vinegar and paint. But the beet juice in some of the large vats would suddenly become sour and no one could understand why. If this problem was not solved, many people would lose their jobs.

4 One of the manufacturers asked Louis to find a solution. Soon, Louis was looking at beet juice very carefully under his microscope.

Make microscope.

He discovered that it was yeast that actually caused the beet juice to turn into alcohol. He also discovered that other microscopic organisms caused the beet juice to turn sour. Now Louis could help the manufacturers by suggesting ways that they could keep the "bad germs" out of the beet juice.

In 1858, Louis Pasteur wrote about all of his findings in a report which he gave to other great scientists. In his report, he suggested that other germs or microbes could be the cause of many of the diseases that made people ill. He said that germs were everywhere, even in the air. The other scientists laughed at him. They made fun of Louis and said he was looking for an "invisible enemy."

5 But Louis did not give up. He kept working until he discovered a way to kill the microbes by heating wine, milk or other liquids that fed the microbes. Today we call this process "pasteurization." Every glass of milk and every serving of yogurt that you eat has been pasteurized, or heated to a high enough temperature to kill any harmful microbes in it.

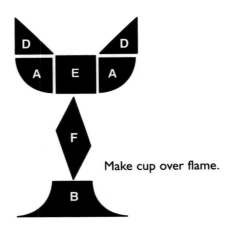

Make cup over flame.

Louis thought that other germs might be causing other health problems. One sickness in particular affected Louis Pasteur and his family very tragically. Two of his daughters died of typhoid fever. Louis desperately wanted to find a way to prevent this from happening again.

6 To scientists and doctors, Louis explained that harmful germs caused many infections. He explained over and over again that specific germs cause contagious diseases. Doctors in hospitals began to listen to him because they were unhappy that 50 out of every 100 patients died after surgery. Many patients seemed to be getting better after an operation, but then, within a few days, they would get an infection and die. Some doctors began washing their instruments in strong solutions to destroy germs as Louis had urged them to do. Medical workers began washing their hands before and after helping a patient.

Make hand.

Before Pasteur's microbe theory, doctors did not know that dirty hands spread germs and made people ill. Once Pasteur's antiseptic methods were used, many lives were saved.

7 Then in 1865, Louis Pasteur was called on again to help many people in France who were in danger of losing their jobs. This time the problem was with silk worms. More and more silk worms were getting sick. The worms could not make the silk threads that weavers wove into beautiful cloth. Pasteur discovered that the silk worms had not one but two microbes inside them causing the problems. With Louis Pasteur's help, the silk makers solved their problem.

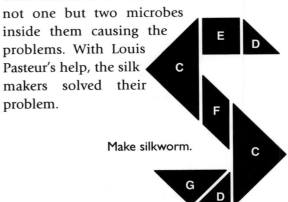

Make silkworm.

8 Pasteur spent many long hours looking at microbes under his microscope and trying to find ways to prevent the diseases that they spread. One disease that he studied was rabies. He had not forgotten the rabid wolf that had bitten his friend Annette so many years ago. After five years of tests and experiments, he finally found a way to vaccinate animals so that they would not get rabies if they were bitten. But he did not want to test his rabies vaccination on a person.

Then, in 1885, nine-year-old Joseph Meister was attacked by a rabid dog that bit him fourteen times. Pasteur was not ready to use his vaccine on people, but Joseph would surely die without it. So over a period of ten days, Joseph got one shot each day with Pasteur's rabies vaccine. It worked!

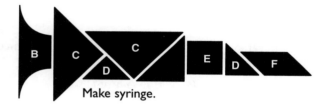
Make syringe.

Joseph's dog bites healed and he did not get rabies. He got well! The entire world was excited by this news.

9 People from all over Europe who had been bitten by rabid animals came to Pasteur's laboratory for his vaccine.

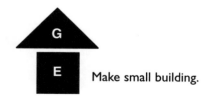
Make small building.

10 Fourteen months after Louis treated Joseph, almost 2,500 people had received Pasteur's vaccine. People donated money to build another, bigger research laboratory devoted to discovering new ways to prevent and treat diseases.

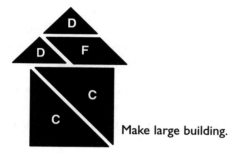
Make large building.

Joseph Meister, the little boy who received the first rabies vaccine, grew up and came to work at the Pasteur Institute, taking care of the buildings.

Raise your hand if you have a dog. Have you ever taken your dog to the veterinarian? When you did, the vet probably gave your dog a rabies shot so that your dog and you would be safe from this disease. And it all started with the big risk that Pasteur took when he gave little Joseph that first rabies shot.

Louis Pasteur continued to work until he was nearly 70 years old. When he became too old to do the actual experiments himself, he explained his ideas to other scientists so that they could continue his research.

Louis Pasteur died in 1895 at the age of 72. Throughout his entire life, Louis never lost his sense of curiosity and wonder. Louis had the courage and imagination to ask different and unusual questions that might lead to a new answer. Louis had the determination to continue to search for the answer even when experiment after experiment failed. All of his life, Louis Pasteur's goal was to use his scientific discoveries to help people get well and stay healthy. Because of Louis Pasteur's lifelong dedication to helping people, he made a difference of one—and what a difference it was!

Activities & Discussion Questions

1. During Pasteur's lifetime, rabies was a serious problem. Learn more about this disease by using the reference books in your library. Some facts you might want to look for could include symptoms of the disease, number of recent cases, ways of transmittal, and how rabies is prevented today.

2. In order to prevent rabies, all dogs are required by law to get a rabies vaccine. Ask how many students have a dog, and how many have taken their pet to get his shots. Discuss how this helps to protect the community.

3. Today, milk products are pasteurized for our protection form bacteria that can cause disease. Look on milk cartons and other dairy products to find the word "pasteurized."

4. Rabies is a disease caused by a virus. Find out more about viruses by using any source that you choose. A couple of possibilities include the Look Out for Germs page (http://www.bms.com/fightinfection/kids/index.htm) which has tips on staying well. There is also MadSciNet (www.madsci.org). This is an interactive science site with a "Ask-A-Scientist" to e-mail for answers. Be sure and check the archives or use the Search option before sending an e-mail question.

Super Search Question

Louis Pasteur was interested in a wide range of scientific questions. In his time, cloning was not even a possibility. Now we have Dolly, the sheep. What does "cloning" mean and who is Dolly? Try the Why Files at <http://whyfiles. news.wisc.edu/034clone/> to get you started.

To learn more about Louis Pasteur

Websites

► Louis Pasteur
http://www.ambafrance.org/HYPERLAB/PEOPLE/_pasteur.html
This website provides biographical information about Pasteur and his discoveries. From Hyperlab. You will need to select the British flag in the upper righthand corner to see this page in English.

► Louis Pasteur and the Pasteur Institute
http://www.pasteur.fr/Pasteur/presentation-uk.html
This website provides links to information about the Institute, Louis Pasteur, the Pasteur Foundation, and the relationship between Pasteur and the United States.

Books

Birch, Beverley. *Pasteur's Fight Against Microbes.* (Science Stories Series). Barrons Juveniles, 1996.

Greene, Carol. *Louis Pasteur: Enemy of Disease.* Children's Press, 1990.

Morgan, Nina. *Louis Pasteur.* (Pioneers of Science). Bookwright Press, 1992.

Parker, Steve. *Louis Pasteur and Germs.* (Science Discoveries). Chelsea House, 1995.

Sabin, Francene. *Louis Pasteur: Young Scientist.* Troll, 1983. Biography of childhood and young adult years. Easy text.

Princess Diana

After Diana's death, one Briton said, "A lot of people are reflecting on themselves, looking at their own lives and how they relate to others. If everyone just smiled at each other and said hello, the way Diana did, the world would be a lot friendlier."

Princess Diana was one of the most beautiful, admired, loved, photographed and talked about women in the world. **(1. Draw arching line to represent world.)**

Some people envied her fairy-tale princess life which seemed easy to them. They saw that she was a beautiful woman with lots of fantastic clothes, tons of money, huge houses, and fancy vacations. Best of all, Diana was going to be Queen of England someday.

What many people did not see was her unhappy childhood, her disappointment in her marriage, the problems that constant attention from the media brought, and her feeling of being a prisoner in her own home, even if it was a palace. Most of all, they did not see all the time and effort that Diana put into helping people.

Princess Diana was a friendly person who made everyone feel as if they knew her and she knew them. She influenced the world in many ways. But she started out as a young girl who struggled with her school work, enjoyed athletics, and was known as an exceptionally kind and helpful person.

When she was only twenty years old, Diana married Prince Charles, Britain's future king, in a fairy-tale wedding in 1981 that captivated the world. Diana herself came from a long line of English nobility. She was used to living a privileged life, but she was not used to photographers following her so closely that she could not even take a walk down the street when she wanted.

In 1982, Diana's first son, Prince William was born. Then in 1984, her second son, Prince Harry was born. She wanted her sons to see what the world outside the palace was like, so she took them to places that you and I like to go to, such as fast-food restaurants and Walt Disney World. At Disney World, they stood in line for the roller coaster ride just like everyone else. **(2. Draw wavy line and crown bottom.)**

When the boys were older, she took them with her to visit shelters for the homeless and AIDS patients. She set a good example for other mothers by being a caring and fun-loving mother.

Although Diana was a princess, she shared the same hopes, dreams and fears that other people have. She showed courage and stubbornness in the face of her own real-life problems, which she shared with the world. She was not afraid to admit her mistakes and then learn from them.

In 1996, Diana and Charles divorced. She was no longer the future queen. She kept the title of Princess and became known as the "People's Princess." She told a television interviewer, "I'd like to be queen in people's hearts." **(3. Draw three hearts.)**

During this time, Diana was helping about 100 charities. She realized that this was too many, so she decided to focus all of her energies on just six of them. These charities were: The Leprosy Mission; The English National Ballet; The National AIDS Trust; Great Ormond Street Hospital for Children; The Marsden Hospital; and Centrepoint, a charity for the homeless. By limiting herself to just six, she could serve these organizations better and hopefully have more time in her private life for herself and her sons.

In January of 1997, Princess Diana joined the campaign to ban the manufacture and use of land mines all over the world. Land mines are small bombs that are hidden in the earth. They blow up when someone unknowingly steps on them. Diana traveled to Angola and visited with victims of these land mines.

Everywhere she went, photographers followed Diana. This bothered her when she wanted privacy, but it helped when she wanted publicity. During her visit to Angola, the entire world learned about the serious problem of land mines and the importance of countries working together to outlaw them forever.

Diana was aware of the power she had to attract attention to people needing help. Everywhere she went, she gave speeches to explain the problems of other people. These are some of the reasons why she was so effective at convincing people to give money to help others. Even small children sent coins to her to be used to help someone in need. **(4. Draw circles.)**

Intuitively, Diana knew how to help people with their pain. There are many photographs of her reaching out to hug someone in need. She said, "I come with my heart, and I want to bring awareness to people in distress, whether it's in Angola or any other part of the world. The fact is, I'm a humanitarian figure. I always have been, and I always will be."

Because the camera of the world was focused on her almost constantly, wherever she went became news. When she attended fund-raising events for charities, the charities themselves also became news. Her presence attracted attention to worthwhile causes that otherwise would not have received the publicity they deserved. Even the clothes she wore helped her causes. She donated 77 of her fancy party dresses to an auction that was held in New York City in June of 1997. The sale of her dresses made over three million dollars for AIDS and cancer charities.

She impressed the directors of the charities with her willingness to work hard and put in long days visiting with sick and poor people. She met with Mother Teresa in India in October 1994. They discussed their mutual interest in charity work. Mother Teresa said, "Diana helped me to help the poor, and that's the most beautiful thing."

Many other directors of charities praised her. "Diana spoke out on behalf of people with AIDS when others wouldn't even say the word. Her commitment will be among her most enduring contributions to the world," said Derek Bodell, director of National AIDS Trust.

On August 31, 1997, when she was just 36 years old, Diana was killed in a car accident in Paris, France. The car that she was riding in crashed in a tunnel. The car was being driven by an allegedly drunk driver, and Diana was not wearing a seat belt.

The entire world mourned this terrible loss. They shed tears for Diana's sons, and also for themselves.

(5. Draw teardrops.) In London, mourners stood in long lines to write messages of love in condolence books.

In life, Diana's humanitarian work helped thousands of people. She contributed both herself and her time. She set an example for others that no one is ever too beautiful, too busy, too rich, or too self-involved with their own problems to help someone else.

In death, her contributions will continue in many ways. The majority of the publishers of books and magazines about Diana have announced that part of their profits will be donated to land mine victims or other charities that she supported. Many other businesses have also made donations in Diana's name.

After Diana's death, people all over the world, who previously had known nothing about Diana's charity work, wanted to do something in her memory. They sent donations to Kensington Palace where Diana had lived. A memorial fund in the princess's name was quickly set up and immediately it became Britain's biggest charity.

Diana's life and her death affected people all over the world. For example, the science students and staff of Clay Junior High School in Carmel, Indiana, sent the following message for inclusion in the book of condolence messages for Diana, in recognition of her unique contribution to mankind:

"Dear Diana, You have opened paths for research and education that no one else could have ever done. Many of our students may not have known you before this sad time, but they are well aware of your achievements now. We are forever grateful for what you have done for mankind and the pursuit of scientific endeavors." **(Untape drawing and fold together to make crown.)**

Diana was given the title of princess when she was a young woman. But during the course of her life she *became* a true princess because of the way she gave of herself to benefit the rest of the world.

Activities & Discussion Questions

1. Princess Diana had six favorite charities to which she devoted her time and energies. These charities are listed in the story. Using the names of the charities or other words associated with Diana's charity work, create a word search or crossword puzzle. You might want to use Puzzlemaker (www.puzzlemaker.com) to help you in this activity.

2. Princess Diana made a lasting impression on the world. Look through the newspaper and find names of notable leaders today. Photocopy or cut out articles about these people. Then choose one leader and write a short paragraph about why you think these leaders will be remembered fifty years from now.

3. Over the years, people have used many adjectives to describe Princess Diana. Make a Character Box by covering a box with paper and then gluing a picture of her on the box. Using markers of different colors, write adjectives, verbs, or character traits about Princess Diana on the box.

4. Princess Diana held a position in society that many people envied. Suppose your were writing a help wanted ad for Princess Diana's job. In your newspaper, find the help wanted section. Read some of these advertisements in order to get an idea of what to include in your job description. In addition to including a description of the fun, glamorous parts of her job, be sure to include the more difficult parts, such as long hours of work and no privacy.

Super Search Question

Select one of the six charities that Diana's Memorial Fund supports and learn more about it. Include the purpose of the organization and who it serves. (The six are: The Leprosy Mission; The English National Ballet; The National AIDS Trust; Great Ormond Street Hospital for Children; The Marsden Hospital; and Centrepoint, a charity for the homeless.)

To learn more about Princess Diana
Websites
► Diana, Princess of Wales
http://www.royal.gov.uk/start.htm

This is the Royal Family's official website. It contains a complete biography of Princess Diana, the Queen's message, details on the funeral arrangements, the order of service, and links to the BBC and the Monarchy websites.

► Diana: A Remembrance
http://cnn.com/World/9709/08/diana.fund.reut/index.html
Key news articles on the death, with information on how to contribute to the memorials. From Reuters News Service.

► Cable News Network Home Page
http://www.cnn.com/
For various articles, search on Princess Diana.

► Angel Hero: Princess Diana
http://www.myhero.com/ANGELS
Short biography of the Princess with links to other sites.

Books
Bach, Julie. *Princess Diana*. Abdo & Daughters, 1990.

Krohn, Katherine E. *Princess Diana*. (A & E Biography). Lerner, 1999.

Licata, Renora. *Princess Diana: Royal Ambassador*. (Library of Famous Women). Blackbirch Press, 1997.

Stone, Tanya Lee. *Diana: Princess of the People*. (Gateway Biography). Millbrook Press, 1999.

Diana: 1961–1997. (pamphlet) Dennis Oneshots Export Limited, 1997.

Articles
"Diana, Princess of Wales." *Biography Today*. Omnigraphics, Inc., 1992.

Chua-Eoan, Howard. "In Living Memory" *Time*. Sept. 15, 1997: 66-75.

James, Martin. "A Tribute to Princess Diana." *Gold Collectors Series Magazine*. Sept.1997.

Masland, Tom. "A Touch of Humanity." *Newsweek Commemorative Issue*. 1997: 62–69.

Reagan, Nancy. "An American Favorite." *Newsweek*. Sept. 15, 1997: 65

For further information:
   The Diana, Princess of Wales Memorial Fund
   P.O. Box 1
   London, WC1B 5HW
   United Kingdom

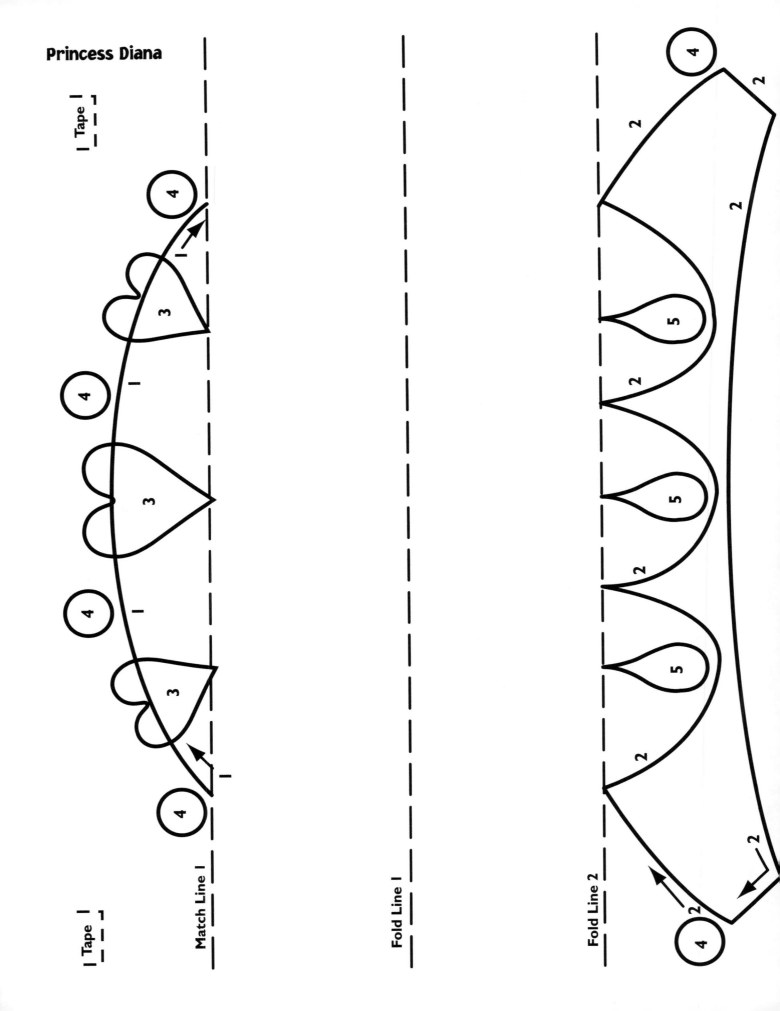

Christopher Reeve

Have you ever heard of Superman? Superman can do everything! Name something that he could do. Yes, that is right. He is especially known for jumping tall buildings in a single bound. **(Draw 1 to 2 to represent Superman jumping over a tall building.)** Superman is a good guy who uses his special powers to help other people.

One actor who played Superman in the movies was Christopher Reeve. He acted in several other successful movies and shows, and he had an incredible future ahead of him.

But, in May of 1995, Christopher Reeve was riding on a horse when he was thrown off. **(Draw from 2 to 3.)** Right away, someone called an ambulance. At the hospital, the doctors did everything that they could to help Christopher. But because he landed on his head, **(Draw from 1 to 4.)** he had fractured a vertebrae in his neck. The nerve cells were injured or disconnected and command impulses could not get from Christopher's brain to the rest of his body. Because of this injury, Christopher Reeve could not walk or move anything but his head.

At first, Christopher felt sorry for himself. But then he decided that feeling sorry for himself was not going to get him anywhere. Instead, he decided to explore his possibilities for improvement and plan what he could do with his life while sitting in a wheelchair.

Christopher has come up with a wide variety of things to do. He participates in a regular exercise program to help his muscles remain strong and flexible. He has also directed a movie made for television and acted in another. **(Draw 3 to 4.)**

But the most important thing that Christopher Reeve has done is to speak out on the need for more money for research into the treatment of spinal cord injuries. Money is needed in order to research ways to restore function to nerves that have been damaged. Scientists believe that there could be several ways to do this. Nerve damage could be corrected chemically, electrically or through a transplant.

There are 90,000 completely paralyzed persons in the United States and 200,000 more people who have spinal cord injuries of some type. This number is increasing due to traffic accidents and sports injuries.

Christopher Reeve is using the fact that his name and face are well known in order to help his cause. He has given many speeches explaining the problems that people with spinal cord injuries have to endure. He asks for donations for medical research. Many research scientists believe that Christopher is responsible for getting Congress to pay greater attention to the issue of spinal injuries. He explains his cause well, and people like him. He is also very determined to make a difference in the lives of people with spinal cord injuries.

Christopher wants to help not just people with his condition, but disabled people everywhere. He is sending a message of hope to the world concerning all disabilities. **(Draw circle, 5.)**

Christopher Reeve, who was 45 in 1999, shared personal a goal. He hopes to be walking by age 50. And he wants researchers to find answers to the problems that he and so many other people face due to spinal cord injuries. In the meantime, he has inspired others with disabilities to take a positive approach to their own disabilities and take charge of their lives. **(Draw circle, 6.)** He says, "When we put our minds to a problem, we can usually find solutions."

Reeve was Superman in the movies, but now because of his determination, he is Superman in real life.

When we see this symbol in parking lots and public places, we can remember Christopher Reeve and the many other people who are meeting the challenges of facing a disability each day. **(Fold line 2 at match line.)**

Activities & Discussion Questions

1. Many schools have a program to teach students about the physically challenged. One program is called "Everybody Counts." At each grade level, children learn about a particular disability. Does your school have this program or a similar one? If not, perhaps you could ask your school nurse to find out about a program in which you and your classmates can learn more about the physically challenged.

2. Superman could do lots of extraordinary things. He used his physical power to help other people. If you were Superman or Superwoman, what would you do to help other people. Draw a picture of yourself as a Superhero helping a person in need. It could be something as simple as lifting up a heavy object that has fallen on someone. Or you could draw a more complicated rescue scene.

3. Christopher Reeve uses the fact that his name and face are well known to help raise money for spinal cord research. You might want to write a letter to the Christopher Reeve Foundation to find out more about it and what you can do to help.

4. Do you think Christopher Reeve is able to use a computer? How do you think the keyboard and monitor might need to be set up so he could use it. Compare your answers with some of the resources listed at the Adaptive Technology Resource Centre website at <http://www.utoronto.ca/atrc/reference/tech/ tech-gloss.html>.

Super Search Question

Try the websites on Superman listed in the resource section. Then see if you can find at least two others on your own. Which is your favorite?

To learn more about Christopher Reeve
Websites

► Christopher Reeve
http://mrshowbiz.go.com/people/christopherreeve/
Celebrity profile on the man and his works, with links to other news articles about him. From ABC News.

► Spinal Cord Research Program
www.uci.edu/~inform/releases/reeve/.html
Home page of the Reeve-Irvine Research Center, which has been founded to study injuries and diseases of the spinal cord with the goal of finding a cure. From the University of California, Irvine.

► Superman Homepage
www.geocities.com/Area51/Vault/7771/index.html
Everything you ever wanted to know about Superman.

Books

Finn, Margaret L. *Christopher Reeve: Actor & Activist.* (Great Achievers). Chelsea House, 1997. Biography includes examples of Reeve's early political and social activism.

Howard, Megan.*Christopher Reeve.* (A & E Biography) Lerner, 1999.

Articles

Daly, Steve. "A New Direction: Sixteen Months After His Accident, Christopher Reeve Switches Roles, From Leading Man to First-Rate Film Maker." *Entertainment Weekly.* November 15, 1996.

Little, Jan. "Christopher Reeve Crusades for $10 Million. Is It Enough for a Cure?" *Accent on Living.* Winter 1996.

Rosenblatt, Roger. "New Hopes, New Dreams." *Time.* August 26, 1996.

Schneider, Karen. "Local Hero: Christopher Reeve Returns to His Hometown" *People Weekly.* January 27, 1997.

"Superhuman Flight: Actor Christopher Reeve Addresses Neuroscience Fundraiser in Toronto, Canada." *Maclean's.* September 16, 1996.

Reeve, Christopher. "America Is Stronger When We All Take Care of Us." Speech given to the Democratic National Convention, Chicago, Illinois, August 26, 1996.

For more information write:
The Christopher Reeve Foundation
P.O. Box 277, F.D.R. Station
New York, NY 10150-0277

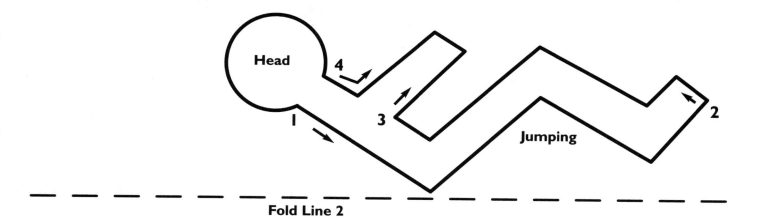

Head

4

1

3

2

Jumping

— —
Fold Line 2

— —
Fold Line 1

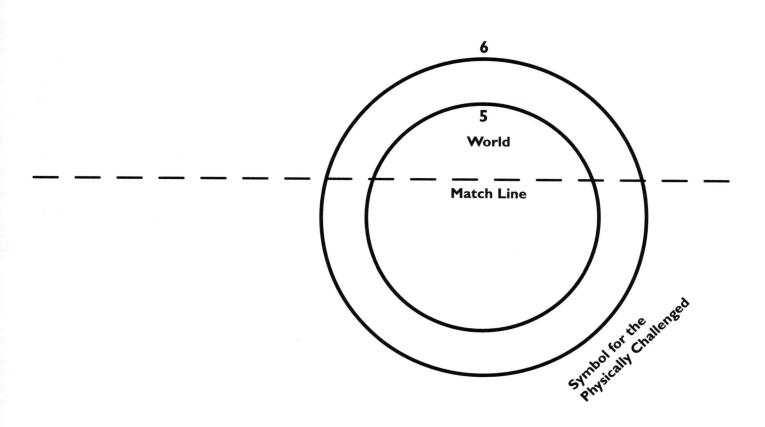

6

5

World

— —
Match Line

Symbol for the
Physically Challenged

Eleanor Roosevelt

Eleanor Roosevelt was a person who, despite many personal problems, dedicated her life to helping other people. She made great efforts to improve housing conditions for the poor, reduce unemployment, win more rights for women, and provide for needy children.

As a child, Eleanor was very rich and could have anything she wanted, but she had nothing she really needed. Just like the rest of us, Eleanor needed love, attention and respect. But she did not have any of these. **(Fold paper in half at line A. Then cut line 1, roof line.)**

Eleanor was shy and timid as a child. She had reason to be withdrawn. Her father, whom she loved very much, had a drinking problem and had been sent away from Eleanor and her brothers. Her beautiful mother called Eleanor "Granny" and made her feel unattractive, unwanted and alone.

When Eleanor was eight years old, her mother became very sick. During her mother's painful illness, Eleanor often sat by her mother's beside and stroked her mother's head to ease the pain. It gave her great satisfaction to know the she was helping. That winter Eleanor's mother died.

Eleanor and her two brothers were sent to live with their grandmother. It was a strict, gloomy household. Tragedy struck again in the spring when Eleanor's little brother Elliot died from scarlet fever and diphtheria. When Eleanor's father died two years later, Eleanor felt really alone. **(Cut opening at line 2.)**

When Eleanor was fifteen years old, her grandmother sent her off to school in England. Eleanor loved school. She would later model many of her ideas after her favorite teacher who taught her that everyone should try and make the world a better place for people who were less fortunate. Eleanor spent three happy years at the school and wanted to stay on, possibly as a teacher. But her grandmother insisted that she return to New York, and so Eleanor had to leave.

Back in the United States, Eleanor was again lonely but kept busy by taking care of her family and teaching dancing and gymnastics to poor children in New York City. When she was nineteen, her distant cousin, Franklin, asked her to marry him. In many ways, Franklin reminded Eleanor of her beloved father because he made her feel attractive and loved.

They were married in 1905. During the first years of their marriage, Franklin's mother was a big part of their life together. She decided where they would live, and even decorated their house for them. She hired someone to do the housework and chose a nanny to help with the children. **(Fold line B, cut opening at line 3.)**

Eleanor was very busy because she had six children! Sadly, one child, Franklin Jr., died of influenza when he was only seven months old. Eleanor did not go out much when the children were small because they needed her time and attention. Between her mother-in-law and her children, Eleanor sometimes felt that she did not have much of a life of her own.

Eleanor's social life changed when Franklin was appointed Assistant Secretary to the Navy. They moved to Washington, D.C., and Eleanor was expected to attend parties and social outings. These official gatherings bored Eleanor and she wished for some real work to do. She soon found it by working as a volunteer helping soldiers who were going off to World War I. She served soup, cheered up lonely soldiers, and supervised women who knitted wool sweaters, socks and scarves for the soldiers.

In 1920, women gained the right to vote, and Eleanor devoted her energy to encouraging women to exercise their voting privileges. She also put effort into improving working conditions for women and speaking out for the rights of children and minorities. **(Fold line C, cut openings at lines 4 and 5.)**

Her husband, Franklin became sick with polio in 1921, and Eleanor nursed him through this difficult time. Franklin's mother thought that he should live a quiet, retired life. But Eleanor convinced him that even though he could not walk, he could still continue his active life.

More and more, Eleanor was becoming confident in her own abilities to think things through, make good decisions, and act on her own. In an effort to make a difference, she became involved in politics. Eleanor also published articles in magazines, started a wood-working factory in order to give people jobs, and ran a private high school for girls. She was an inspiring teacher and took her students on field trips all over New York City to help them learn about people different from themselves..

When Franklin became governor of New York, Eleanor used this opportunity to improve state prisons and hospitals. She traveled widely and became known as a person who cared about people's problems and tried to do something about them.

Starting in 1932 and for three full presidential terms, Eleanor lived in the White House with Franklin. During her years there, she changed the role of First Lady. Before Eleanor became the First Lady, the wife of a president was expected only to give parties, and act as a hostess for social events. But Eleanor did more than that. She continued to work for social welfare and reform. She spoke over the radio about things that concerned all Americans. Her talks made Americans feel that they had a friend in the White House. During World War II, she traveled many miles, comforting wounded and homesick soldiers. **(Fold line D, cut openings at lines 6 and 7.)**

When Eleanor was 61, her husband, President Franklin Roosevelt, died. After his death, Eleanor

decided that she should retire. But the world still needed her. The new president, Harry Truman, asked Eleanor to represent the United States at the first meeting of the new United Nations in London, England. This was an opportunity for Eleanor to work for world peace. She traveled all over the world, convincing people that world peace depended on world friendships made up of mutual respect and understanding.

Eleanor kept busy with her activities until her death in 1962 at the age of 87. Her funeral was attended by the President, two former presidents, and a future president. The entire world mourned the death of a woman who had overcome her shyness and dedicated herself to improving conditions for people everywhere. One statesman, Adlai Stevenson, said of her, "She would rather light a candle than curse the darkness. And her glow has warmed the world."

Eleanor Roosevelt lived for twelve years in the most famous house in the nation, the White House. **(Unfold and show White House against background color.)** From the White House she reached out to help countless others.

Eleanor Roosevelt used her intelligence, compassion and influence in politics to improve the world. She was only one person—yet she made a huge difference.

- -

Activities & Discussion Questions

1. Eleanor Roosevelt lived at the White House for twelve years. Find out more about this famous house by using the resources in your library or take the tour at the White House website (whitehouse.gov/WH/glimpse/tour/html/index.html .

2. Draw a comic strip of Eleanor Roosevelt's life. Use three to six boxes. You may use any incidents from the her life but be check to make sure that they are in chronological order.

3. The U.S. has been enriched by its First Ladies, and this story is about one of the greatest of these women. Select another First Lady from the White House website (http://www.whitehouse.gov/WH/

glimpse/firstladies/ html/firstladies.html) an Internet site to learn more about. Check your school library to see if you can locate further information there.

4. The story mentions that women were first granted the right to vote in 1920. Why do you believe it took so long for women to be granted this right? Where could you find more information about the struggle to win this right, and learn about the individuals who worked for women this right?

Super Search Question

Many famous men and women are well remembered for the inspiring words they have said or written. Eleanor Roosevelt is a good example of such a leader. Using resources in the library (such as *Bartlett's Familiar Quotations*) or an Internet source find a quotation from Eleanor Roosevelt that you like; copy it and your source.

To learn more about Eleanor Roosevelt
Websites

► Eleanor Roosevelt, 1884–1962
http://www.fdrlibrary.marist.edu/bioer.html
A brief biography and timeline are provided here for both Eleanor and Franklin along with further information and links on the Roosevelt presidency.

► Eleanor Roosevelt Center at Val-Kill
http://ervk.org/
Home page for the Eleanor Roosevelt Center which continues to pursue Eleanor's philosophy of purposeful action. Select "Related" from the menu at the bottom of the page for additional Web links.

► The First Ladies – Eleanor Roosevelt
http://www.whitehouse.gov/WH/glimpse/firstladies/html/ar32.html
A biography of Eleanor Roosevelt with a link back to information about other first ladies. From the White House website.

Books

Adler, David A. *A Picture Book of Eleanor Roosevelt.* Holiday House, 1991. Simple, brief biography for primary students.

Clinton, Susan Maloney. *First Ladies.* (Cornerstones of Freedom). Children's Press, 1997.

Cooney, Barbara. *Eleanor.* Viking, 1996. Reading level ages 4–8.

Faber, Doris. *Eleanor Roosevelt: First Lady of the World.* Viking, 1985.

Freedman, Russell. *Eleanor Roosevelt: A Life of Discovery.* Clarion, 1993. Written for young people, this is a biography of one of the greatest first ladies, including photographs, a bibliography, and information on Eleanor's life after FDR's death.

Kulling, Monica. *Eleanor Everywhere: The Life of Eleanor Roosevelt.* (Step Into Reading (Library)) Random Library, 1999. Emphasizes how Eleanor overcame her shyness and childhood fears.

Sabin, Frances. *Young Eleanor Roosevelt.* Troll, 1990. Recounts Eleanor's early life.

Eleanor Roosevelt

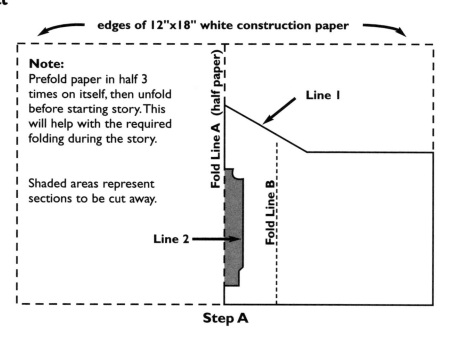

Step A

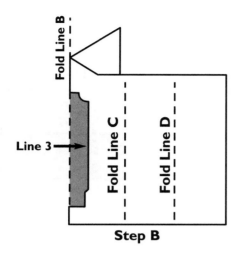

Fold Line B

Line 3 →

Fold Line C

Fold Line D

Step B

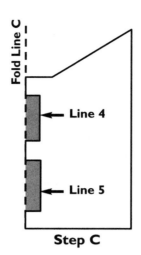

Fold Line C

← Line 4

← Line 5

Step C

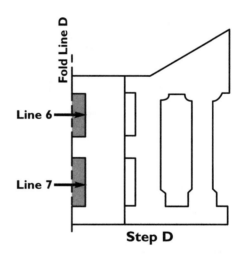

Fold Line D

Line 6 →

Line 7 →

Step D

Place White House over 12"x18" blue or black background paper.

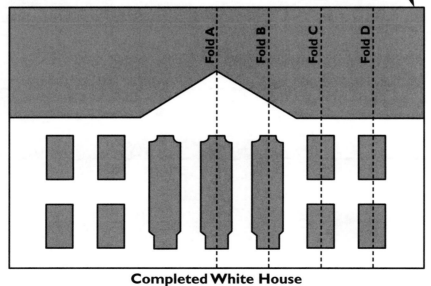

Fold A

Fold B

Fold C

Fold D

Completed White House

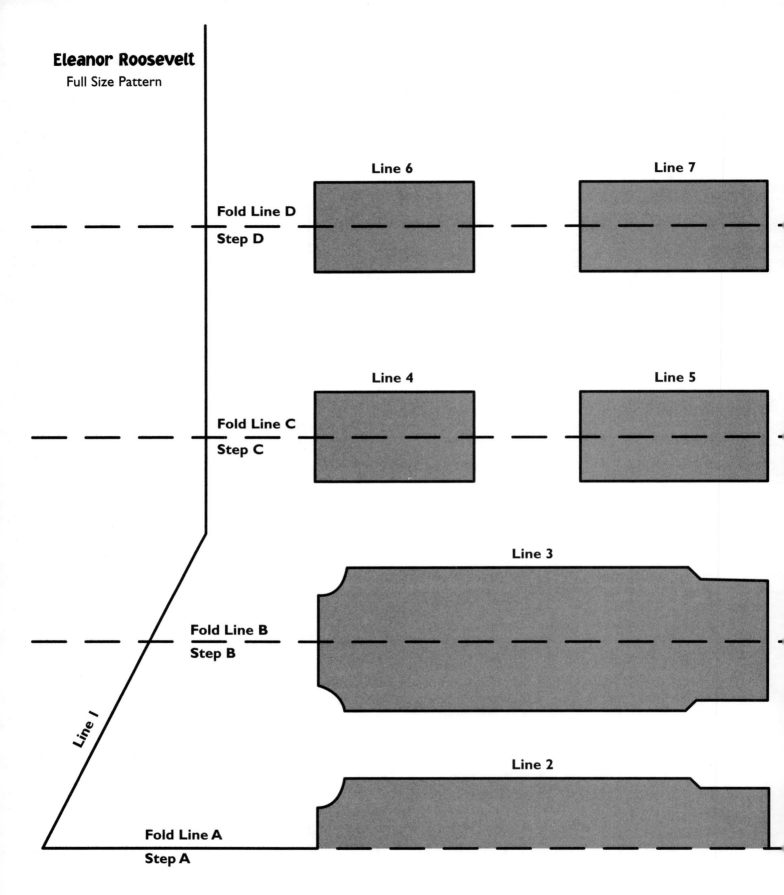

Eleanor Roosevelt
Full Size Pattern

Line 6

Line 7

Fold Line D

Step D

Line 4

Line 5

Fold Line C

Step C

Line 3

Fold Line B

Step B

Line 1

Line 2

Fold Line A

Step A

Albert Schweitzer

1 Albert Schweitzer's daughter said that her father's life helped make people "aware of what just one person's actions can accomplish in our troubled world." Here is the numeral one to represent the importance of one person.

Make "one."

2 Albert Schweitzer was born in 1875 and died in 1965. He was a very talented musician, writer, teacher and minister. But Albert Schweitzer was more than all these things. He was a man who devoted himself to serving humanity. As a young man, Albert started out with an unusual plan for his life. Albert told himself that he could do anything that he wanted to do until he was 30 years old. When he reached that age, he would dedicate the rest of his life to helping needy people in the world.

Add world.

Here is how it all began:

Have you ever hurt another person or an animal? Maybe it was an accident or maybe you did it without thinking, but you probably felt badly afterwards. That's what happened to Albert when he was ten years old.

Albert was playing a game with his sister Adele. He wanted her to play better, but she could not or would not. Albert got so frustrated that he angrily hit her in the face. Immediately Albert felt horrible. He asked himself how could he do such a cruel thing?

3 This was not the first time that Albert felt awful about harming another person or an animal.

When he was seven, Albert's friends asked him to go bird hunting with them.

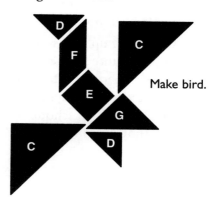

Make bird.

Albert did not want to go. But he also did not want his friends to laugh at him or call him names. So he went with them. The boys crept up to a tree full of birds and got their sling shots ready. Just as they were all about to shoot at the birds, the church bells began to ring. To Albert, the ringing of the bells seemed like a personal message just for him. Instead of using his sling shot, Albert quickly stood up and yelled as loudly as he could. He waved his arms madly about, shooing the birds away.

Albert made up his mind that day that he would never kill or hurt any living thing, just for the sake of doing it.

This was the beginning of Albert Schweitzer's philosophy or way of thinking about life. Later on, he called it "Reverence for Life." By this he meant that all life is special and every living thing has a right to live. Albert wrote several books explaining his ideas.

4 Another thing that helped Albert form his thinking was a statue of several Africans. One man in the statue looked beautiful but so sad.

Make sad face.

Albert said, "His face, with its sad expression, spoke to me of the misery of Africa." Albert's feelings toward the African in the statue would lead him many years later to Africa and his life's work. (By the way, the statue that so impressed Albert was created by Frederic Auguste Bartholdi, the same sculptor who created the Statue of Liberty in New York Harbor.)

Albert grew up in Alsace, a town on the border between France and Germany. Throughout his childhood, Albert did better and better in school. He also excelled at playing the organ. After he graduated from high school, Albert went to college to study religion and philosophy, which means ways of thinking. He became a preacher and a school principal. He also wrote books and was a famous musician. Albert was great at everything he decided to do.

While he was in his twenties, Albert started searching for a way that he might help the world when he turned 30 years old. For him, it was hard to be happy when so many other people in the world were unhappy.

After reading a report about the people of Africa, and remembering his strong feelings for the statue of the unhappy black man, Albert decided that helping in Africa was what he should do. His friends and family did not want him to go—Africa was so far away. It was a country of heat, disease and malnutrition. Besides, they asked, how could Albert help people? He was a famous writer, teacher, philosopher and musician. How could these talents help?

5 Albert did not let anything stop him. He enrolled in medical school at age 30. Eight years later, Albert was a doctor. He married and left a few months later with his wife, Helene, for the African country of Gabon. He was happy and excited.

Make happy face.

6 When Dr. Schweitzer arrived at the mission of Lambarene, he expected to find a hospital. But he did not. Instead he found only an old chicken coop. He had no choice but to clean up the chicken coop and use it as both a hospital and a house in which to live.

Make chicken coop.

Dr. Schweitzer did find many people who needed his help. They suffered from malaria, eye problems, sleeping sickness, leprosy, skin diseases, snakebites or injuries from wild animal attacks. Dr. Schweitzer worked from early morning until late into the evening performing operations, administering medicines, and supervising every aspect of his ever-growing hospital community.

For 50 years, Albert Schweitzer devoted his time, energy and money to help sick and injured people. He also traveled throughout Europe giving organ recitals and lectures about his philosophy of "Reverence for Life."

7 Although it was never his goal, Albert Schweitzer became famous throughout the world. He won many awards and prizes. One of the greatest prizes was the Nobel Peace Prize, which he received in 1952. True to his dedication to helping others, he used the money from this prize to build a hospital just for leprosy patients. Over the years other dedicated doctors and nurses joined him in Africa.

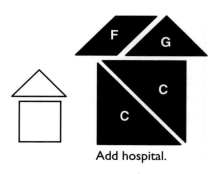

Add hospital.

In 1949, Dr. Schweitzer traveled to America. Everywhere he went, he received honors and praise. Americans were impressed with his accomplishments, but they were even more impressed with Albert himself. Albert was just himself—friendly, open, sincere, kind and funny. Americans liked his "Reverence for Life" idea because it appealed to their own pioneer spirit, courage and sense of community. To Americans, Dr. Schweitzer was a hero.

8 Albert Schweitzer wanted to help the people of the world by warning them of the dangers of nuclear weapons. He wrote and spoke to as many people as he could about this new danger to all the peoples of the world. Just as he had saved the birds in his childhood, Albert wanted to save people from nuclear disaster.

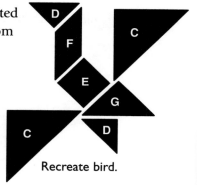

Recreate bird.

For the remainder of his life, Dr. Schweitzer worked as hard as ever helping thousands of Africans in his hospital. Without Albert's dedication, these people would likely have never seen a doctor or received medical attention. He died in 1965 at the age of 90, a much admired and loved man.

Throughout his life, in countless ways, Dr. Albert Schweitzer made life better for people everywhere. Today, there are many hospitals and relief organizations all over the world named after Dr. Schweitzer. They are all striving to follow his example by helping sick and needy people.

Countless individuals have also been inspired by Dr. Schweitzer's life to develop their own "Reverence for Life." They try to follow his advice to be "kind and simple." Dr. Schweitzer said, "Wherever a man turns, he can find someone who needs him."

Dr. Schweitzer dedicated his life to helping other people and proved that one person can make a difference.

Activities & Discussion Questions

1. Albert Schweitzer won a Nobel Peace Prize in 1952. There have been many other Nobel winners. Visit the official Nobel website (http://www.nobel.se) and find the list of laureates, or past winners. Select one of these to learn more about.

2. Albert Schweitzer's motto was "Reverence for Life." How did he practice this belief? If you believed in this philosophy, how would you seek to apply this belief today? What career would you select that would offer the greatest opportunity to benefit others?

3. Dr. Schweitzer traveled to Africa to open a hospital. Today doctors and nurses are still needed in Africa and other developing countries. Design a help wanted advertisement for these positions. Include a job description, and several phrases about why this would be a rewarding job.

4. Dr. Schweitzer's advice to people all over the world was to be "kind and simple." This is much like the advice that Mother Teresa gave. She said, "Do small things with great love." With a friend make a list of small, simple things that you can do today to help someone else. For more ideas, go to http://www.actsofkindness.org.

Super Search Question

Where did the idea for the Nobel Prizes come from? *(Answer: Alfred Nobel, a chemist, industrialist and the inventor of dynamite, left directions in his will that much of his fortune was to be used in the award of annual prizes for physics, chemistry, physiology or medicine, literature, and peace. The first was awarded in 1901.)*

To learn more about Albert Schweitzer

Websites

► The Albert Schweitzer Page
http://www.pcisys.net/~jnf/
An extensive selection of links to sites on all aspects of Dr. Schweitzer's life and philosophies.

► The Nobel Prize Internet Archive: Albert Schweitzer.
http://nobelprizes.com/nobel/peace/1952a.html
Information on Dr. Schweitzer's nomination for the award with extensive links to other Internet resources, books by and on Dr. Schweitzer.

► International Albert Schweitzer Foundation
http://www.schweitzer.org/
Home page for the foundation with information about the life and work of Dr. Schweitzer.

Books

Bentley, James. *Albert Schweitzer: The Doctor Who Devoted His Life to Africa's Sick.* Gareth Stevens, 1991.

Greene, Carol. *Albert Schweitzer, Friend of All Life.* Children's Press, 1993.

Johnson, Spencer. *The Value of Dedication: The Story of Albert Schweitzer.* Oak Tree, 1979.

Knauer, Kelly, ed. *Great People of the Twentieth Century.* Time, 1996.

Lantier, Patricia. *Albert Schweitzer.* Gareth Stevens, 1991.

Robles, Harold. *Albert Schweitzer: An Adventurer for Humanity.* Millbrook, 1994.

Thomas, M.Z. *Albert Schweitzer.* John Knox Press, 1964.

Sequoyah

Have you ever heard of the giant trees in California that have been living and growing for several thousand years? They are called Sequoia trees. They were named in honor of an American Indian called Sequoyah. He invented an alphabet for his people so that their culture could endure just as the trees have endured for so many years.

Over 200 years ago, when Sequoyah was a young boy growing up in Tennessee, he discovered that he was good with his hands. He had a special talent for drawing. But Sequoyah did not draw on paper because he did not have any paper. With a stick, he drew in the soil. He drew what he knew and loved; the animals of the forest.

Sequoyah could pick up a stick and quickly draw a bird. Soon Sequoyah was collecting pieces of bark to draw on. He could also carve interesting animals and birds out of bits of wood.

Sequoyah amazed his friends with his artwork. This helped Sequoyah feel more accepted. Because for most of his life, he had suffered with a lame leg and walked with a limp. He could not run races and play ball games with the other boys. In fact, the name Sequoyah means "the lame one." His art ability helped to make up for his lameness.

He made beautiful spoons, buttons, and jewelry out of melted silver. Then he drew designs and pictures of birds or deer in the silver. Sequoyah's people loved wearing the beautiful jewelry that he made and the traders were anxious to buy his crafts.

When the white traders stopped by his Cherokee Indian village, Sequoyah traded his artwork for the things that he and his mother needed to live. Sequoyah's father had been a white trader and Sequoyah's mother taught him all that she had learned from him about trading with the white man.

After Sequoyah's mother died, he felt sad in the home where they had lived for so many years. So Sequoyah decided to move. He chose Alabama. There Sequoyah built his own cabin and workshop. He worked as a blacksmith and mended things for peo-ple. He also got married. **(Cut from 1 to 2, half cir-cle.)**

But as Sequoyah went about his busy life tending his house, garden, and workshop, an idea was growing in his mind. He dreamed of wanting to put down in picture words all of the Cherokee language. When he spoke of this idea to the other Cherokees, some of them laughed.

Many of his friends believed that there was a magic power in books. They called the book the "white man's talking leaves." Sequoyah explained that it was not magic, just a system of making marks on a "leaf." Do you know what a "leaf" is? Yes, it is a piece of paper. But it is easy to see why they called the thin pieces of paper "leaves," isn't it?

Sequoyah was determined to make his own talking leaves. He wanted the power of the talking leaves for his people. If the Cherokee had their own language, then they could store knowledge and use it again and again as the white men had done. Also, if the wonderful stories that the medicine men told on special occasions were written down, then the Cherokee could enjoy the stories any time they wished.

Sequoyah thought about a system of writing more than ever after he became a soldier in the American army in 1812. He worked as a blacksmith for the army in Georgia. At night, Sequoyah noticed that the white men took out their "talking leaves." Sometimes they would look at the marks and then talk to their friends about them. Then, they got out new, clean "leaves" and made marks on them. They sent these off to their families. The soldiers also received "talking leaves," which were letters from their families. In this way, the white soldiers knew what was happening with their families, while Sequoyah and his friends had not heard anything from their families for almost two years. What do we call this system of looking at marks on a piece of paper and then making new marks on a piece of paper? ....Yes, reading and writing. **(Cut from 3 to 4.)**

More than anything, Sequoyah wanted to give his people the power to read and write. After the war of 1812 ended, Sequoyah returned home to his wife and young daughter. But his wife soon became angry with Sequoyah because he spent all his time writing strange pictures on sheets of bark. When Sequoyah tried to explain to his wife and friends what he was doing, they did not understand and called him a fool.

At first, Sequoyah tried to make a picture for every Cherokee word. But after a few months, he realized that this system would not work. There were too many words and each word had several meanings.

It seemed to Sequoyah's wife that Sequoyah was always too busy making his strange markings to take care of the cabin and the garden. One day, in anger and frustration, his wife picked up all of his bark sheets with the pictographs on them, and threw them in the fire. In one angry moment, Sequoyah had lost all of his work. Depressed, Sequoyah took his youngest child and moved to a abandoned cabin several miles outside his village. His marriage was over and it seemed that his work was over also.

But in the middle of this terrible event, a miracle occurred. Sequoyah's daughter found a book that had been dropped by a white man. Not knowing what it was, she gave it to her father.

By studying the marks in the book, Sequoyah realized that there were only 26 marks, and that they were used over and over. We call these…yes, "letters of the alphabet," don't we? Sequoyah soon learned that the marks were put together in endless different combinations to make….yes, words. Then he realized that the words were put together to make…yes, sentences.

Now Sequoyah understood that the letters represented a sound and not a word. The sounds were put together in different combinations to make words. Sequoyah developed 86 symbols representing all the sounds made in the Cherokee language. Some of the symbols he borrowed from the white man's book. He also created some of his own letters.

But Sequoyah's neighbors did not understand Sequoyah or what he was trying to do for them. They were frightened of him and his daughter. One day, while no one was at home, they set fire to Sequoyah's cabin. Once again, all his work was lost.

But like his first loss of his bark sheets, this loss proved to be the next step in Sequoyah's work. He decided to move farther west to Arkansas. On the way, Sequoyah met a woman who understood his dream.

They married and she and her son helped Sequoyah and his daughter simplify and perfect the Sequoyah's Cherokee symbols.

At last, Sequoyah was finished with his project and he could now write any word using the letters in his Cherokee alphabet. He decided to travel east and show his work to the Tribal Council in Tennessee. The Cherokees in the east were known as the Eastern Cherokee Nation.

Sequoyah's daughter went with him and together they showed the group of Cherokee leaders how Sequoyah's strange markings worked. At first, they did not believed that Sequoyah could make certain marks on a paper to represent what he said. They were even more amazed that later his daughter could look at the marks and tell what Sequoyah had said. But after several tests, they understood and they all wanted to learn how to write their name and the names of their family.

Sequoyah and his daughter stayed for a year and taught their people how to use Sequoyah's alphabet. Almost everyone learned how to read and write. They wrote the new letters on everything; the fence rails, sides of houses, tree bark and rocks.

Then Sequoyah traveled back home to the Western Cherokee Nation. He brought with him letters that the Cherokees of the Eastern nation had written to their friends and relatives of the Western Nation.

During this time, when Sequoyah was working on the alphabet, he was also working for peace between the Americans and the Cherokee. He made two trips to Washington, D.C., to help work out land treaties between the United States government and the Cherokee Nation. Later on, he helped the two Cherokee Nations work out their differences when they both settled on the same land reserved for their tribe in Oklahoma.

Sequoyah continued to promote his invention. Sequoyah's alphabet was easy to learn and use. It caught on so fast that a newspaper was printed in the Cherokee language. This was the first Indian newspaper in a native tongue to be published in America. Books were also printed using Sequoyah's alphabet.

Sequoyah was a hero to his people. They gave him an income of $500 a year. This made Sequoyah the first person in the United States to receive a literary prize. The Cherokee Nation Legislative Council also gave him a special medal which had a picture of two peace pipes crossed. **(Cut from 4 to 5. Open out and show pipes.)** The two pipes stood for the two Cherokee Nations united by Sequoyah's written language. **(Unfold paper medal and hold up over black paper.)**

Because of Sequoyah's life-long struggle to find a way to preserve the ancient customs and culture of the Cherokee, the Cherokee language and culture is preserved. Today the Cherokee language is still spoken in many homes and the ancient ways are not forgotten.

Sequoyah's invention of the Cherokee alphabet was a truly amazing feat because he did it all by himself. No one else in the history of the world had ever invented an entire alphabet alone. Sequoyah was only one person but yet his contribution to the Cherokee Nation was invaluable.

Activities & Discussion Questions

1. Sequoyah was a Cherokee. Use your library's print or CD-ROM encyclopedia to locate information about this American Indian tribe, then try one of the websites that describes the history of this tribe (http://www.dickshovel. com/Cherokee1.html). Ask the children to compare the two resources, and summarize the differences.

2. Sequoyah's Cherokee alphabet contains 86 symbols, compared to the 26 letters in our alphabet. Using one of the Internet search engines, locate a copy of Sequoyah's alphabet. A recommended site is (http://www.geocities. com/SoHo/Museum/4786/ cher-keys.htm). Can you follow the instructions and learn how to say thank you in Cherokee. *(Answer: wa-do)*.

3. During World War II, the U.S. used American Indians from the Navaho tribe as radio operators during battle operations against the Japanese. Why do you think that was done? Where would you look to find out more information about this experience?

4. Have you ever written a message to a friend in a secret code? An easy way to make a code is to assign a number to every letter of the alphabet. Make two copies of your secret code. Keep one for yourself and give one to a friend. Then write each other secret messages.

Super Search Question

Sequoyah felt strongly about preserving the language and stories of the Cherokee Nation. Where did his people first live? Where do the majority of them live now? One source for this information is the Official Site of the Cherokee (http://www.cherokee.org/).

To learn more about Sequoyah
Websites

► Sequoyah
http://www.powersource.com/gallery/people/sequoyah.html
A brief biography with information on the Cherokee alphabet.

► Sequoyah Birthplace Museum
http://www.monroecounty.com/museum.html
A description of the Sequoyah Museum with photographs, hours of operation, and information on the surrounding area.

Books

Klausner, Janet. *Sequoyah's Gift: A Portrait of the Cherokee Leader.* HarperCollins, 1993. Biography includes a map, places to visit and further resources.

Oppenheim, Joanne. **Sequoyah: Cherokee Hero.** Troll, 1979.

CD-ROM

"Cherokee Language." *Microsoft Encarta.* Microsoft, 1998. CD-ROM

"Sequoyah." *Microsoft Encarta.* Microsoft, 1998. CD-ROM.

Sequoyah

Note:
Cut circle and pipes out of white or gray paper. Hold round "medal" against black background paper.

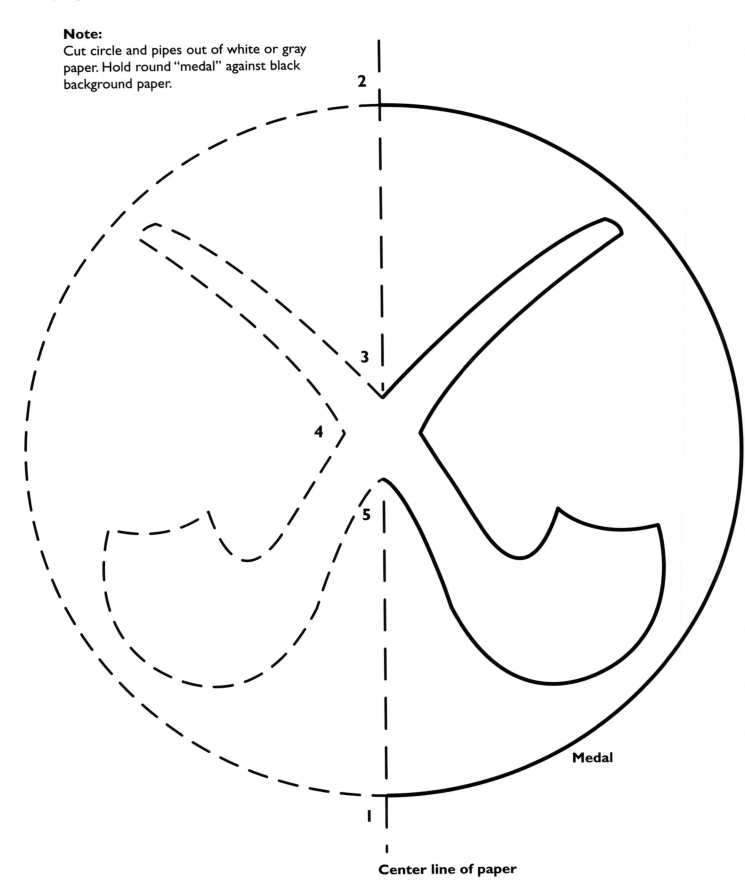

2

3

4

5

1

Medal

Center line of paper

Harriet Tubman

Frederick Douglass wrote to Harriet Tubman, "The midnight sky and the silent stars have been witnesses of your devotion to freedom and of your heroism."

Harriet Tubman's life is a story about one person's bravery and courage in the face of great danger. It is also a story about many people helping and sharing during times of great danger. Finally, Harriet Tubman's life is a story about numbers, as you will learn.

1820: This is the year that Harriet was born in Maryland. **(Begin at top of page. Write down 1820.)** She was the sixth of eleven children. They all lived in a hut with a dirt floor. It had no windows and no furniture. As soon as she was born, Harriet was owned by Mr. Edward Brodas, the plantation owner who owned Harriet's mother and father. They were slaves of Mr. Brodas. Today, slavery is illegal, but back in 1820 (Indicate number again.) white people were allowed to own people who were originally from Africa.

As a slave child, Harriet was allowed to stay with her mother at night. "Grandmother," a slave who was too old to work in the fields, took care of Harriet and several other small children during the day while Harriet's mother and father and her older brothers and sisters worked in the fields.

7: (Write 7 under 1820.) That's how old Harriet was when she put a bandanna around her head and went to work on a nearby farm. Slaves wore bandannas around their heads to show that they were old enough to work. Harriet went to work for Miss Susan, but Miss Susan did not know how to teach Harriet how to do her jobs. Miss Susan often whipped Harriet instead of explaining. One day, Miss Susan told Harriet to sweep the floor and dust the furniture. Harriet knew how to sweep, but her hut did not have any furniture so she did not know how to dust. Miss Susan whipped Harriet for her ignorance. Even when Harriet was an old woman, she still had those scars from the whipping.

Miss Susan was wrong to treat Harriet this way, and she was wrong to use slaves to do her work. Many people thought that owning slaves was wrong. All across the United States, concerned citizens argued against slavery. They wanted to abolish, or get rid of slavery. Even though Harriet could not read, (because it was against the law for slaves to learn to read and write), she knew about this movement by listening to people talk about it.

15: (Write 15.) Harriet was fifteen years old when she got hit in the head by a heavy weight. It happened when another slave was trying to escape. He ran into the village store and Harriet followed him. The slave's owner chased the escaped slave. He told Harriet to help him catch the slave but she refused and instead, blocked the doorway. In anger, the man picked up a two pound piece of lead and threw it. The weight did not hit the black man who was running away. Instead, it hit Harriet right in the middle of the forehead. She was knocked unconscious.

Harriet was unconscious for several weeks. She finally recovered, but there was a dent in her forehead and a scar. As a result of this injury, Harriet would have "sleeping fits" for the rest of her life, where she would suddenly fall asleep anytime, anywhere. Then she would wake up just as if nothing happened and continue on with what she had been doing. She would even have a sleeping fit in the middle of a sentence.

24: (Write 24.) Harriet married John Tubman when she was 24. He was a free black man. John was free because his parents had been freed from slavery before he was born. She lived with him in his cabin. Even though she was married, Harriet was still a slave.

1849: (Write 1849.) This was the year that Harriet escaped. The first time she escaped, she was with three of her brothers. But after they had started their journey north, her brothers became afraid and they all decided to return before anyone discovered that they were gone. Two days later, Harriet heard that she had been sold to an owner in the deep South. Harriet did not want to be forced to move so she decided to run away again.

Harriet wanted her husband John to come with her, but he did not want to go. So Harriet went alone. She traveled by night and hid during the day. She walked 90 miles. When she arrived in the state of Pennsylvania, she was free.

People all along the way helped her. These people were part of the Underground Railroad. The Underground Railroad was not really underground nor was it a railroad. It was a system of houses where runaway slaves could hide and rest during their journey to freedom.

3: (Write 3.) This was how many people Harriet rescued from slavery the very next year after she made it safely to Philadelphia. She knew that by agreeing to help rescue slaves, she was in great danger of being caught and punished. The first three people she helped were her sister, and her sister's two children. They were about to be sold down South and Harriet rescued them just in time.

19: (Write 19.) This is how many trips Harriet made to rescue slaves and, as she said in her own words, "I never ran my train off the track and I never lost a passenger." Harriet even rescued her own parents.

$52,000: (Write 52,000.) This is how much reward money was offered to anyone who could capture Harriet. But she was never caught and the $52,000 was never paid to anyone.

1861: (Write 1861.) The Civil War began and Harriet helped in many ways. First, she was a nurse in a military camp hospital. She helped both escaped slaves and wounded soldiers. Then she led 300 black soldiers on three gunboats up a river to rescue 800 slaves in South Carolina. Harriet helped by serving the Union army as a spy and a scout. Everyone she met admired her courage and willingness to risk her life in order to help win freedom for black people everywhere.

1865: (Write 1865.) The Civil War and slavery finally ended in 1865. But Harriet's service did not end. Harriet went home to care for her elderly parents in Auburn, New York. She also wanted to help start schools for black children and a home for the elderly. Many former slaves came to her door for help. Some were hungry, some were too old or too sick to work. These people needed rest, food and even clothing. Harriet always helped everyone who asked.

How did she get her money to help so many people? She sold vegetables from her garden to her friends and neighbors. When Harriet came around with her vegetable basket, they hoped she would not only sell them some vegetables, but also tell them a story. They all loved listening to Harriet's stories about her Underground Railroad trips and her adventures as a spy in the army.

Harriet not only helped black people, she also helped all women. How? Harriet supported the right for women to vote. She did all that she could so that all women could vote in elections.

1908: (Write 1908.) This was the year that Harriet's dream of a home for elderly and sick blacks came true. The home opened and Harriet herself, now an old woman, moved in three years later.

1913: (Write 1913.) On March 10, 1913, Harriet died of pneumonia. She was 93 years old. She was given a military funeral and the entire town came to pay their last respects to Harriet.

Harriet Tubman was a woman who spent her life fighting battles for freedom. She wanted people to be free from slavery, free from hunger, free from homelessness, free from sickness and free from disease. She was not powerful and she was not wealthy, but she was able to give much to others.

All of these numbers add up to *one*—one woman whose courage and bravery and selflessness added up to helping hundreds of other people. **(Draw a line and write the numeral one under it.)** Harriet Tubman was one person who made a difference.

Activities & Discussion Questions

1. Learn more about Afro-Americans and their history by researching this topic on the World Wide Web. An interactive treasure hunt can be found at Black History, Past to Present (http://www.kn.pacbell.com/wired/BHM/AfroAm.html).

2. Harriet Tubman used many different disguises as she went about her rescue mission. If you were to disguise yourself so that you could go on a rescue mission with Harriet Tubman, what would you dress up as? Draw a picture of yourself in your disguise. Remember to check your drawing carefully to make sure that you have not drawn an electronic wristwatch, a battery operated toy sticking out of your pocket, or other things that were not invented in Harriet's time.

3. Harriet Tubman was not the only person who worked for freedom for her people. Use the resources in your library to research Sojourner Truth, Frederick Douglass, and others.

4. Slavery in the U.S. ended with issuance of the Emancipation Proclamation, but discrimination against African Americans and other cultural groups has continued. Why do you think this occurs? What do you feel can be done about it?

Super Search Question

Using the resources below, find out when and where the Underground Railroad operated? Write a one paragraph summary of your findings.

To learn more about Harriett Tubman & the Underground Railroad

Websites

► Harriet Tubman and the Underground Railway
http://www2.lhric.org/pocantico/tubman/tubman.html

A learning activity for 2nd grade students. From the Pocantico Hills School.

► Lifesaver Hero: Harriet Tubman
http://www.myhero.com/directory/index.html
Select "Lifesavers" and then Harriet Tubman to find a biography and links to other sites.

► Resources for Harriet Tubman
http://artsedge.kennedy-center.org/student/harriet.html
An extensive listing of links to resources on Harriet Tubman and the Underground Railroad.

Books

Adler, David A. *A Picture Book of Harriett Tubman.* Holiday House, 1992. Biography with brief, simple text for primary readers.

Bains, Rae. *Harriett Tubman: The Road to Freedom.* Troll, 1990. Reading level is YA.

Benjamin, Anne. *Young Harriett Tubman.* Troll, 1992.

Haskins, Jim. *Get on Board: The Story of the Underground Railroad.* Scholastic, 1997. Introductory history includes personal stories about individuals who were involved in the Underground Railway.

Lawrence, Jacob. *Harriet and the Promised Land.* Simon & Schuster, 1997. Narrative illustration with rhythmic verse by African-American artist for Gr. 1–3.

Levine, Ellen. *If You Traveled on the Underground Railroad.* Scholastic, 1993. Question and answer format. Reading level ages 9–12.

McClard, Megan. *Harriett Tubman.* Silver Burdett, 1991.

Taylor, M.W. *Harriett Tubman.* Chelsea House, 1991. Biography with interesting details.

Harriet Tubman

1820	Born
7	Started Work
15	Injured
24	Married
1849	Escaped
19	Rescue Trips
$52,000	Reward
1861	Civil War Started
1865	Civil War Ended
1908	Tubman House
1913	Died

equals **1** (one) Person

Raoul Wallenberg

Raoul Wallenberg was a man who stopped death with passports. A passport is a special piece of paper that allows you to travel freely from one country to another. For the Jewish people captured by German soldiers during World War II, these passports were tickets to freedom. Raoul Wallenberg saved the lives of thousands of Jews with his special passports. This is the story.

Raoul Wallenberg was born on August 4, 1912. The Wallenbergs were one of the most well-respected and privileged families in Sweden. Members of his family were bankers, sailors and diplomats. Unfortunately for baby Raoul, his father, a naval officer, died three months before he was born. A few days before his death, Raoul's father said to his mother, "I would be so happy if only our little baby grows into a kind and good human being." Raoul's mother promised that she would do her best.

It seemed that travel and passports were to be a way of life for Raoul Wallenberg. Raoul's grandfather, Gustav, directed Raoul's education. He wanted Raoul to have a broad education, so he saw to it that Raoul spent time in Germany and France to learn the language and culture of these countries. Raoul also learned to speak English and Russian.

Gustav became the ambassador to Turkey. When Raoul was only eleven, he used his first passport to travel alone to Turkey to visit his grandparents. **(Fold yellow paper at line A.)**

Ever since he was a little boy, Raoul was always interested in the construction of buildings. When he became college age, Raoul wanted to study architecture. Raoul once again used his passport to travel to the University of Michigan. He was a very good student and won the respect and admiration of his professors and fellow students.

During school vacations, he traveled all over the United States by hitchhiking. He knew it wasn't safe, but Raoul thought it was a great opportunity to practice diplomacy and negotiating. One day, when he was on his way back to school in Michigan, he was robbed by four men with whom he had gotten a ride. After they took his money, they threw him into a ditch. Raoul later wrote, "I did not feel any fear the whole time. It was more like an adventure." Raoul's lack of fear would be very helpful later on in his life.

After graduating in three and half years from the University of Michigan, Raoul used his passport to travel to Cape Town, South Africa, where he worked for a business owned by friends of his grandfather. **(Fold paper in half again on fold line B, see shaded area on direction sheet.)** Then he used his passport to travel to Palestine (which is now Israel) to work in a bank there. Raoul's grandfather wanted Raoul to learn all he could about business and banking because Gustav wanted Raoul to open a world bank with him.

After Raoul had worked in the bank for awhile, he wrote to his grandfather and said, "I am not cut out for banking. I think I have the character for positive action, rather than to sit at a desk and say 'No' to people."

Raoul returned home from working in the bank and soon found a new job in which he used his passport often. As Raoul traveled all through Germany on business in the early 1940s, he learned that the Jewish people were persecuted unfairly. They were forced to leave their homes and move to other countries. Jews were forced to wear badges so that everyone would know they were Jewish. They could not own property, businesses, or send their children to school. **(Cut at line 1.)**

Raoul became more and more disturbed by this, especially when he learned that the German Nazi leader, Adolf Hitler, had set out to kill all the Jews in Europe.

By 1944, leaders from countries all over the world knew that Hitler was planning to massacre the large Jewish community in Hungary. The president of the United States, Franklin D. Roosevelt, set up an organization called The War Refugee Board. This group of leaders decided that they needed to send someone to Budapest, Hungary, to help the Jews. But the United States could not send someone from America because we were at war with Germany. They secretly asked the neutral country of Sweden for help. When the Jewish leaders of Sweden were asked who they thought would be qualified for this dangerous mission, Raoul's boss recommended him.

Raoul immediately accepted the job but on his terms. He said that he must be free to do whatever he could to save lives. Raoul wanted to use any method that he saw fit. Because time was running out, Raoul wanted to be able to make decisions on his own without checking each time with Swedish officials. He wanted enough money to rent houses and buy food for the Jews who had been thrown out of their homes. The king of Sweden himself approved Raoul Wallenberg's unusual demands. Raoul left for Budapest immediately and arrived there on July 9, 1944. There he found 230,000 Jews trapped by the Nazis in this city.

Adolf Eichmann, one of Hitler's men, was planning to kill all of these people, and *soon*.

Wallenberg knew he had to work fast. The first thing he did was print a Swedish passport that looked very impressive and official. He used his architect's training to design the passport in yellow and blue. Yellow and blue are the colors of Sweden. The triple crown of Sweden and lots of official signatures were printed in four different boxes. **(Cut at line 2. Open paper and place over plain blue paper. Show listeners.)** This passport was called a Schutz-Pass or Protection Pass. It looked very official, but it was really nothing but a fake.

Raoul was given permission to give out only 1,500 of these passports, but he gave out over 20,000. The fake passports saved many lives. But more than that, diplomats from other countries learned from Raoul. They also began making their own fake passports and handing them out to the Jewish people. If a person had a passport, they were allowed to go free. Many times, after a passport had allowed one Jewish person to go free, Raoul would give the same passport to another person. So one passport sometimes saved many lives. When Raoul ran out of time to print the fancy yellow and blue Schutz-Pass, he used regular paper to make more passports. These passports also saved many lives.

Raoul set up hospitals, orphanages, and soup kitchens to feed people. He rented houses for the Jewish people. **(Cut roof at line 3. Place over blue paper with predrawn or photocopied faces. Show listeners.)** Raoul bought medical supplies, food, and clothing with his own money and money supplied by the United States. He knew that he would be killed if the Germans ever found out that he was working with their American enemies.

Still, Raoul was unafraid and worked with great skill and energy. He allowed himself only four hours of sleep a night. He had a staff of 400 people to help him. They worked in shifts—so that someone was always there working to save people's lives.

Raoul said to his workers, "Help everyone you can. If you have a problem, call me. But, most important, you must treat each person like a human being. The Nazis try to tell the Jewish people that they are worthless, that they are dogs, and that there is no hope. We must remind them that they are important. They are people. There is hope. The Nazis have given power to evil. We will give power to good."

From July 9, 1944, until January 17, 1945, Raoul Wallenberg worked heroically to save as many people as he could because he knew that each person was important.

In January 1945, the Soviet army entered Budapest and the German threat to the Jewish people ended. On January 17, 1945, Raoul Wallenberg left Budapest for a meeting with Soviet officials in another town. He wanted to discuss his plans for helping the Jews after the war.

Unfortunately, Raoul Wallenberg never returned. Over the years, several former prisoners of the Soviet Union stated that they saw him in the Soviet prisons, but Soviet officials never gave out any information about Raoul. His death became a great mystery.

In 1981, Raoul was made an honorary citizen of the United States of America. President Ronald Reagan said, "In the depths of the horrors of World War II, Raoul Wallenberg was one shining light of inspiration, upholding the honor of the human race." Raoul Wallenberg and his Schutz-Pass won the admiration and the hearts of freedom-loving people everywhere.

Whether he was killed or put in jail, we will probably never learn the real truth about what happened to Raoul Wallenberg. **(Fold paper at line C to illustrate jail with bar in windows. Place over blue paper and show listeners.)**

But we do know that Raoul was one ordinary person who showed extraordinary courage in standing up for his beliefs. He left a safe home in Sweden for a dangerous rescue mission. He did what he could to help other people. He was one person and yet he saved the lives of over 100,000 people during World War II.

Activities & Discussion Questions

1. Raoul Wallenberg dedicated his life to saving refugees during World War II. Unfortunately, with every war there are people who are displaced from their homes. Using news magazines, or newspapers, or the *New York Times* Online (http://www.nytimes.com/learning/) look for articles about people who are now refugees due to war, famine, or other catastrophes.

2. Raoul Wallenberg gave out fake passports to Jewish people so that they could escape. Learn more about passports. What is a passport and how do you get one today? When do you need one? Then ask your relatives if they have a passport. Perhaps they could show it to you and tell you about the places that they have traveled.

3. Throughout history there have been many instances of persecution against people who had different religious beliefs. Why do you think this occurs? What can be done to reduce or eliminate this discrimination in the future?

4. In this story about Raoul Wallenberg, we learned that he did many things to save people's lives, including some things that broke the law, such as printing fake passports. This is an example of "the ends justify the means." How do you feel about this? When do the ends not justify the means?

Super Search Question

The official Raoul Wallenberg website (http://www.raoul-wallenberg.com/) is written in four different languages. What are they?

To learn more about Raoul Wallenberg

Websites

► The History Place: Holocaust Timeline
http://www.historyplace.com/worldwar2/holocaust/h-wallen.htm
This site contains the passport photo of Raoul Wallenberg and a summary of his life and work.

► Raoul Wallenberg
http://www.raoul-wallenberg.com/links/links.html
The official Raoul Wallenberg website with links to other Internet resources.

Books

Bierman, John. *Raoul Wallenberg: Righteous Gentile.* Viking, 1996. Biography for young adults.

Billings, Henry, and Melissa Billings. *Heroes: 21 True Stories of Courage and Honor.* Jamestown, 1985.

Daniel, Jamie. *Raoul Wallenberg: One Man Against Nazi Terror.* Gareth Stevens, 1992.

Linnes, Sharon. *Raoul Wallenberg: The Man Who Stopped Death.* Jewish Publication Society, 1994. Biography with black and white photographs.

Nicholson, Michael. *Raoul Wallenberg.* Gareth Stevens, 1989.

Smith, Danny. *Wallenberg: Lost Hero.* Templegate Publishers, 1987.

For more information write to:
Raoul Wallenberg Committee
Jan E. Muller
443 C West Grant Place
Chicago, IL 60614

Raoul Wallenberg

Note:
Standard weight colored copy paper
is the easiest to fold and cut.

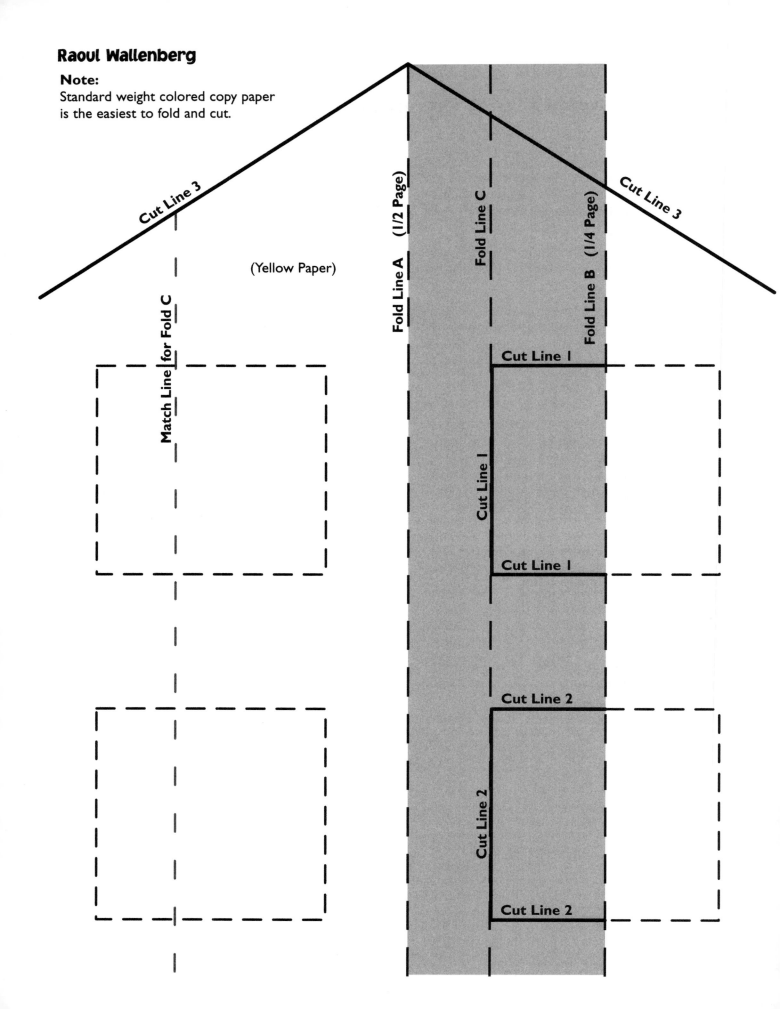

(Yellow Paper)

Cut Line 3

Cut Line 3

Match Line for Fold C

Fold Line A   (1/2 Page)

Fold Line C

Fold Line B   (1/4 Page)

Cut Line 1

Cut Line 1

Cut Line 1

Cut Line 2

Cut Line 2

Cut Line 2

(Blue Paper)

Story Method Directions

Why Combine Storytelling with These Hands-On Methods

Telling a story while cutting, drawing, signing, or creating a puzzle picture is a great way to completely capture your listeners' interest. These are unusual approaches to story-telling and your story will have lots of action. Most children love to cut, draw, play with puzzles or learn sign language. After hearing one of your stories, your students will want to use these same methods to create their own stories.

Also, when speaking in front of a group, most people feel more confident if they have something to do with their hands. These methods fulfill this need.

Do you need to be an artist, seasoned storyteller, or have special training in sign language?

No! All you need to do is photocopy the drawings, signs, or puzzle pieces.

How can you and your students create original stories?

1. Decide on a story to tell, then choose an object that is an integral part of the story. Or, choose the object first and then create the story involving that object. For the paper-cutting and mystery-fold methods, objects to be drawn should be symmetrical. For the sign language stories, choose several favorite words from your story to sign. When using the story puzzles, encourage the children to use their imagination to create figures to go with their stories. "How to draw" books (available in most libraries) are a great resource for ideas.

2. Students may wish to work with a partner. One partner tells the story and the other partner does the cutting, drawing, signing, or creates the puzzle figures.

3. This is a great time to teach the elements of a story. Every story needs the following: an introduction, characters, location or setting, action or plot, and resolution or ending.

4. Expect a wide range of drawings and stories from your students. Their stories might even be remarkably similar to one have told. That's great and quite a compliment to you.

5. Encourage students to tell their stories with their partners first and then to another friend. They may want to put their story in writing, make a story web, or outline. When they tell their story to you, you can help them refine it.

6. After several practices with small groups of friends, your storytellers will be ready to present to the rest of the class. After their presentation, you might want to give each child a "Storyteller's Certificate" or tell another story yourself.

Mystery-Fold & Storyknifing Stories

What is Mystery-Fold?

Drawing and folding the "answer" to a story out of a piece of paper is a unique way to tell a story, and it yields an unusual surprise for the listener. It is also a great way for children to learn to tell stories.

As you tell these stories, you will be drawing on both the left and right sides of the paper. The drawing lines are related to the plot. At the end of the story, the object is completely drawn. During the last sentence of the story, you fold the paper together to reveal the "answer." After you tell a few Mystery-Fold stories, your students will be telling and folding their own tales.

What is Storyknifing

'Storyknifing is an intriguing name that is based in history. In the late nineteenth century, anthropologists and ethnologists discovered that the Inuit people told stories to each other while drawing pictures in the winter snow and summer mud. To draw their pictures, they used a rounded knife made of whalebone. Their method of storytelling came to be known as storyknifing.

As you tell these stories you will be drawing a picture. Today you can use markers, chalk, or crayons! At the end of the story, you will also have completed a drawing to share with your listeners.

How do you get started telling Mystery-Fold and Storyknifing stories?

1. First place a piece of white paper over the pattern in the book. With a pencil, trace all drawings lines very lightly. (Later on, you might let your listeners in on this secret.)

2. A basic Mystery-Fold is done by folding the paper in half across the width of the paper, then folding it in half again. Make this fold parallel th the first, which will divide that paper equally into four long rectangular sections. Return to the first fold, and fold the end rectangular section back

onto the adjacent one. Now only the two end sections are visible; the middle two sections are not.

In storyknifing, you are just drawing on a piece of paper.

3. During the telling, relate the drawing steps to the story-line. For example, as a character goes places or does things, add new lines to your picture.

4. Practice telling your story while drawing so that it becomes natural to talk and draw at the same time. Becoming familiar with the story and the drawing allows you to present the story easily and develop a natural rapport with your listeners.

   If you feel the picture will be easily guessed while you are telling the story, draw your picture upside down or sideways.

5. If you forget what comes next or get stuck in a story, ask the listeners to repeat what's happened thus far (giving you time to think) or suggest what could come next.

   After hearing a few stories, children will begin to try to figure out the object you are drawing before you fold the drawing together. You will know by a child's facial expression when he or she knows what it is that you are drawing. If you notice a listener just bursting to tell the answer, recognize him or her quietly with an aside such as "Shhh…it's a secret."

   When you are storytelling with a large group, you will want to tape the drawing paper to a wall or chalkboard. You can enlarge the picture with an opaque projector to make it more easily seen. Drawing on chart paper also works well. Use the lines to help you keep the two halves lined up properly. If you have just a few listeners, everyone could sit around a table.

6. Retell the story at least once. Retelling the story gives the listener a second chance to enjoy it as well as to learn the story and the drawing steps. Stories can and should be changed by each storyteller, and a story will be a little different each time it is told.

 ## Sign Language Stories

Why sign language?

Sign language is as beautiful as a ballet. Add it to a good tale, and you've got a winning combination. You will find it works well with many stories, and listeners can immediately join in on the repetitive words or phrases, making the story-telling more exciting for everyone.

Having mastered a few signs, children will develop an appreciation and understanding of sign language, and its role as a commonly used language throughout the world. Millions of people with a hearing loss use sign language because it's a very effective way of communicating. Today a hearing loss does not prevent people from achieving their goals.

This book's intent is to use signs to enrich the story-telling experience. Because the signs are used in isolation, in some cases, they do not reflect the linguistic rules of sign language. The stories are not dependent on the signs.

How do you get started telling sign language stories?

1. Choose your story and read it over several times. Practice the signs that go with the story.

2. During your telling of the story, sign words only as often and as quickly as you feel comfortable. Trying to sign all the words repeatedly the first time you tell the story can be difficult. The signing should not slow the story down or affect your delivery. Signing a greater number of words will become easier after you tell several stories. You will be surprised at how quickly you pick this up.

   For purposes of clarity, all of the words that have signs appear in boldface type throughout the story. You will want to choose how often you do a particular sign.

3. Decide how you want your listeners to be involved. The story that you select helps determine the way you involve the listeners. Here are several possibilities:

   • Children can listen to you and watch you do the signs as the story unfolds.

   • All the listeners can do the repetitive phrase with you.

   • Individuals or groups of children can "be in charge" of a word, and sign their word each time it is mentioned in the story.

4. While you are telling the story, you may wish to have this book open on your lap. This makes it very easy to refer back to the signs or story at any time.

5. Retell the story at least once. Retelling the story gives the listener a second chance to enjoy it as well as to learn the story and the signs. Stories can and should be changed by each storyteller, and a story will be a little bit different each time it is told.

 ## Paper-Cutting Stories

What is Paper-Cutting?

Cutting the "answer" to a story out of a folded piece of paper is a unique way to tell a story, and it yields an unusual surprise for the listeners. It is also a great way for children to learn to tell stories. The stories are short, easy to tell and deceptively simple.

As you tell these stories, you will be cutting an object out of a folded piece of construction paper. At the end of the story, the object is completely cut out and unfolded. The paper-cut object is an integral part of the story.

After you tell a few of these stories, your students will soon be telling their own paper-cutting tales both at home and at school. Some children will bring stories to school that they have made up at home; this generates enthusiasm in other children to do the same thing.

How do you get started telling Paper-Cutting stories?

1. Photocopy the pattern from the book. If you want to transfer the cutting lines to colored paper, then cut out your white pattern, place it on the colored paper and trace around it.

2. Practice telling your story while cutting so that it becomes natural to talk and cut at the same time. Cutting steps are related to the story. As the character goes somewhere or does something, you cut a new line. Becoming familiar with the story and the cutting allows you to present the story easily and develop a natural rapport with your listeners. When you are not cutting, just hold the paper and scissors naturally or put them down if you want to gesture while talking.

   If you forget what comes next or get stuck in a story, ask the youngsters to repeat what's happened thus far (giving you time to think) or suggest what could come next.

3. Retell the story at least once. Retelling the story gives the listener a second chance to enjoy it as well as to learn the story and the cutting steps. Stories can and should be changed by each storyteller, and a story will be a little bit different each time it is told.

Story Puzzle Stories

What Are Story Puzzles?

Story Puzzles are a variation of tangrams. Tangrams are wonderful ancient Chinese puzzles that are still used today by children and adults. Each tangram consists of a square which is cut into seven pieces. (Tan means piece.) Pictures can be created with these pieces. All seven pieces must be used. They must touch but no pieces may overlap.

I really liked these puzzles and wanted to involve children in using them to tell their own stories. However, my students and I discovered that the requirement to use all seven pieces was difficult for us. Also, we wanted pieces with curves so that we could make pictures of a flower, or the sun in a less abstract manner. I added three pieces on each end of the tangram puzzles which gave us a total of thirteen pieces.

How do you get started telling story puzzle stories?

1. Become familiar with the story you want to tell. Copy and cut out the puzzle pieces. There are two sizes so that you can choose the size that works the best for you.

2. Practice moving the pieces around so that you can easily make the figures suggested in the diagrams. Keep the book open to the story and diagrams so that you may refer to them quickly and easily.

It is really fun to show action with the pieces. For example, lightning (piece F) can strike a tree (pieces C, G, D) and the tree can break apart (scatter pieces around). Students can actually fly their spaceship across their paper, flipping down the wings enroute. A child can make a flower wilt by moving the pieces down a bit.

Show a day from sunrise to sunset by moving the sun (circle of A pieces) across the page. Make a face and show sadness by using your fingers to trace the path of tears down the face.

In summary. you may show action by sliding, folding, coloring, taping, ripping, wadding up, blowing or covering up the puzzle pieces.

3. If you are telling to a small group, you can all sit in a circle. Tell your story as you move the puzzle pieces around on a large piece of poster board or construction paper. Choose the color of the background paper to coordinate with your story.

4. To further enhance your story, you may color or draw on the back of your pieces. For example, color the two large triangles to make butterfly wings. You may cover the pieces with construction paper, tape them together, or fold them to give a three-dimensional look. If you are telling to a larger group, you may wish to use the overhead projector.

   You may wish to create more permanent puzzle pieces cut from cardboard or foam core. Puzzle pieces can be used on flannelboards or metal dry marker boards with applied backings of flannel/Velcro or magnetic tape, respectively.

5. In this book, the pieces have been shaded or coded to indicate the type of action you will take with each piece in the step-by-step illustrations. This makes it easy to see which pieces to add or remove as you tell the story.

How can you integrate story puzzles into the curriculum?

1. Give each student a copy of either size of the puzzle pieces. Have them cut the pieces apart. (I give each child an envelope for storing their puzzle pieces.)

   It is easy to copy extra sets of puzzle pieces. If your students color a set for one particular story, they will need a new set for their next story. Sometimes students will use more than one complete set for their story. You may give your students as many copies of puzzle pieces as they need for their different stories!

2. Let the students play with the shapes. Encourage them to use their imagination and be open-minded. They should not let preconceived notions hamper their creativity. Many times students will get story ideas from the figures they create with their pieces. One student explained to me that he wanted to write a story about a fox because "that's what the triangles kept making themselves into." Have the students write their stories, using an outline, web, or narrative format.

Science and history: Use the story puzzle pieces to represent objects or ideas in science and history. You could make a kite when telling the story of Benjamin Franklin's famous experiment during a thunderstorm. A microscope made from the puzzle pieces will spark students' interest in several different concepts you introduce. A ship or canoe graphically demonstrates a story about explorers and their adventures. A simple house might represent the building where the signing of an historic document took place.

Math: If you are teaching a geometry unit, you will want to involve you students in learning to identify a parallelogram, triangle, square, and polygon. You could ask them to draw these shapes, and then identify them using the puzzle pieces.

Challenge them to make objects with their pieces. Which pieces are symmetrical? Where is the line of symmetry? Can you put several pieces together to make a different, yet symmetrical shape?

You and your students will be making objects that are representational. But also have fun constructing more abstract objects that come right out of your imagination! Tell your listeners about your abstract object as your story unfolds.

In many stories, you will need a majority of the pieces to construct your next picture. Remove the current picture before beginning your new picture. You could also work with two or more sets if you wish to create several pictures.

A	B	C	D	E
F	G	H	I	J
K	L	M	N	O
P	Q	R	S	T
U	V	W	X	Y
Z	0	1	2	3
4	5	6	7	8
9	10			

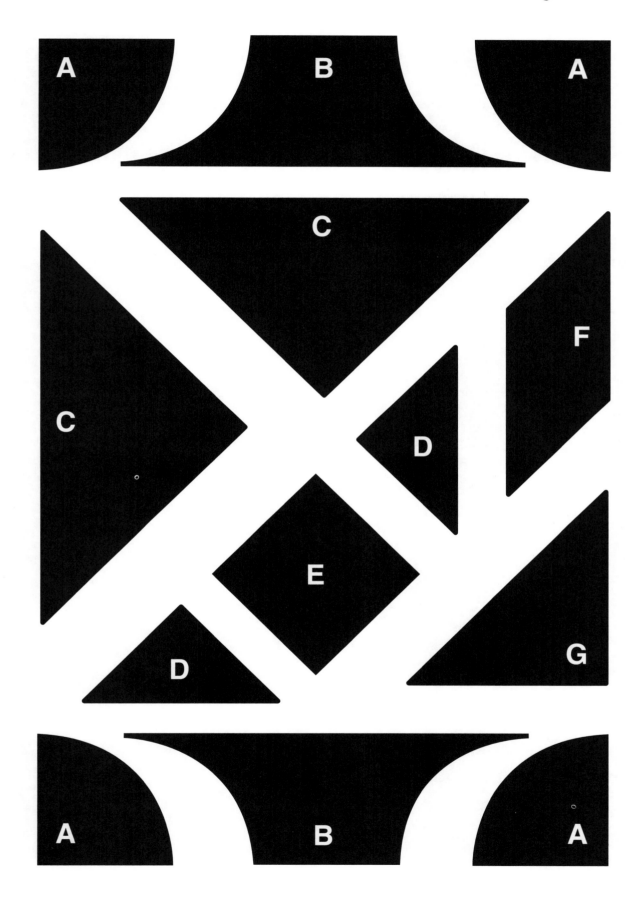